NatWest Small Business Bookshe

This series has been written by a team of
experience and are still actively involved in the day-to-day
small business.

If you are running a small business or are thinking of setting up your own business, you have no time for the general, theoretical and often inessential detail of many business and management books. You need practical, readily accessible, easy-to-follow advice which relates to your own working environment and the problems you encounter. The books on the NatWest Small Business Bookshelf fulfil these needs.

- They concentrate on specific areas which are particularly problematic to the small business.
- They adopt a step-by-step approach to the implementation of sound business skills.
- They offer practical advice on how to tackle problems.

The author

Karen Lanz has many years' management experience. She is at present the personnel and training manager to a small but growing business. She also acts as a consulting director to another company in the small business sector.

Other titles in this series

A Business Plan
Starting Up
Selling

NatWest Small Business Bookshelf

Hiring and Firing

Employing and Managing People

Karen Lanz

Pitman

Pitman Publishing
128 Long Acre, London WC2E 9AN

First published in Great Britain in association with the National Westminster Bank, 1988

British Library Cataloguing in Publication Data

Lanz, Karen
Hiring and firing.
1. Great Britain. Small firms. Personnel management – Manuals
I. Title II. Hollinshead, Graham
658.3'03

ISBN 0-273-02826-X

Printed and bound in Great Britain at The Bath Press, Avon

Contents

To Mum and Dad who taught me about people, to Steve who taught me about business, and to everyone who is struggling to combine the two.

Preface

I have written this book with the practising small business manager in mind. It is by no means meant as a personnel textbook but highlights the practical implications and problems that employing people brings to your business.

You have turned to this book for many reasons. You may be thinking of employing staff for the first time or you may already employ staff and are experiencing problems or are trying to avoid them. I hope that when you turn to the chapter of the book that is most relevant to you at the moment and find it useful, you will then turn to the other chapters of the book and share the practical hints each has to offer.

Your time is valuable, so I'll let you begin reading.

Acknowledgements

I would like to acknowledge the following people who have helped me write this book: Graham Hollinshead, Senior Lecturer, Thames Polytechnic for his input, advice and support; Helen Beltran, Freelance Publisher, for her invaluable help and guidance.

Karen Lanz
March 1988

1 Introduction

One of the most important concerns for small businesses today is that of people. The emphasis is on having the right people in the right place at the right time. The payroll is normally the single biggest overhead a small business has to maintain and so the management of payroll – and therefore people – can be seen as critical to the success or failure of a small business. Unlike large organizations, the loss of a single member of staff can have major repercussions on the small firm.

This book has been written to help owners and managers of the small firm to overcome these problems. There have been many studies on various aspects of personnel but to date there are few that have considered the problems that are peculiar to small businesses.

At first, when the business is small, there are few problems to overcome, but as the business grows, more and more aspects and problems of being an employer come to light. For the purposes of this book we have examined six major areas in turn and looked at the practical implications of each to the small business. We have given examples of how to overcome problems using systems and model letters developed for small businesses. These areas include the hiring of staff, drawing up the contract of employment, the payment of staff, the training of staff and parting with staff. Two other important areas that have been included are the development and application of people-management skills for individuals in small businesses.

Throughout the book, the importance of employment law is examined in each area. In recent years this has had a substantial effect on the relationship between the employer and the employee. The main acts that have been passed are the Equal Pay Act 1970 (amended 1983), the Sex Discrimination Act 1975, the Race Relations Act 1976, the Employment Protection (Consolidation) Act 1978 and the Employment Acts of 1980 and 1982. These acts have given individual employees a number of important statutory rights. If an employee considers that any of these rights have been infringed by an employer or another party, he or she may under certain circumstances make a claim to an industrial tribunal.

The effect of such a legal position on the employer/employee relationship has indeed been substantial. It has affected the power relationship between the two, increasing the employee's power and diminishing the employer's power. The later acts of 1980/1982 have reduced the collective powers of the trade unions. Studies on the employment protection legislation have shown that a secondary function of the law has been to make employers more careful in the recruiting and shedding of labour. The law has attempted to regulate the way in which the 'contract of employment' between employer and employee is reached and terminated and in doing so gives enforceable legal rights to both parties. The law has in fact regulated the dealings of employers with each employee, ensuring that the employer acts *fairly* and without *bias*.

By using case studies and examples and a proliferation of model letters this book shows the employer not only the effects of this area of the law on the business but also ways of dealing with employees so that he or she acts within the law. The law is however continually changing and it is therefore important that new legislation, and its interpretation by the courts, is brought to the attention of the employer and employees as soon as possible. There are many organizations who have developed employment law 'manuals' which are continually updated and have proved invaluable to businesses. This book does not attempt to be a replacement for a legal manual. It is therefore suggested that a copy of such a manual is obtained and used in conjunction with the book. A particularly concise and easy-to-use manual is *Croner's Reference Book for Employers* and is published by Croner Publications Ltd. A copy can be obtained by writing to:

Croner Publications Ltd
Croner House
173 Kingston Road
New Malden
Surrey
KT3 3SS

Many problems arise because they are either not foreseen or because early problems have not been tackled soon enough. This book emphasizes how to approach problems, and highlights the effects of not facing such issues will have on the small business. This book is therefore for the practitioner not the theorist and will help overcome the problems of employing people to allow managers time to concentrate more fully on the business in hand.

2 Hiring

The problems □ The expenses □ Questions to ask yourself □ Do you need anyone else? □ What type of person do you need? □ How do you get people? □ How do you choose the right person? □ Making an offer □ Acceptance of offer

It is important that the small firm gets the recruitment decision right. The effects of poor recruitment will be felt very quickly, and it may lead to problems such as low productivity, low morale and high labour turnover.

The problems

Small firms can experience some particular difficulties, when recruiting:

- inability to match going rates
- inability to offer promotion (offering a 'job' rather than a career)
- requiring more from the prospective employee than a larger firm might
- appearing as an exclusive 'club', particularly in the family firm
- lack of time and resources to devote to recruitment.

On the other hand, you can offer the new recruit a more friendly working environment and increased scope for exercising discretion and responsibility.

The expenses

It should also be remembered that hiring can be an extremely expensive business. Costs include:

- preparing and placing advertisements
- stationery, postage and typing costs
- training costs for apprentices and trainees.

There are also less obvious costs:

- staff time spent on interviewing
- below-standard level of performance from the new recruit during the 'settling-in' period
- wage or salary costs of a poor performer, should the wrong person be recruited.

It is therefore essential that recruitment is based on effective planning to ensure that unnecessary panic measures are avoided, and that the new recruit will be fully occupied at work.

Questions to ask yourself

Before starting to look for someone, you should ask yourself the following questions:

- Do we *need* anyone?
- If so, what type of person?
- How do we get people?
- How do we pick the right person?

Do you need anyone?

You should first consider whether or not you really need to replace a leaver or open a new job. Various other cost-effective options exist.

The recruitment decision

Non-recruitment	Redistribution of tasks within existing workforce
Non-replacement	Flexible working Internal transfer/promotion Use of sub-contractors Overtime working
Part-replacement	Hiring of part-timers Hiring of casual staff or temps Job sharing
Full replacement	Direct replacement Redefinition of job

Non-replacement options

Opt for flexible working

Through encouraging remaining staff to work harder or to cover extra tasks, previous levels of output can be matched. This could save a considerable amount of money, and staff may welcome the opportunity to take on more responsibility.

Transfer staff or promote internally

The benefit of this approach lies in the fact that the employee is already familiar with company practices, and the company is aware of the employee's strengths and weaknesses. The existence of promotion prospects should also serve to motivate employees coming through the ranks. On the other hand, the decision could demoralize other workers who expected promotion, and it may create a need to recruit at a lower level. It could also be the case that the promoted employee performs less well in the new job than he or she did in the previous one. This approach should therefore be used with care, tact and discretion. You should talk to staff that have been overlooked and explain your reasons wherever possible to avoid demotivation.

Use sub-contractors

Engaging sub-contractors may reduce or remove the firm's liability for payment of tax, sickness benefit and pensions, and for the provision of holidays and maternity leave. The firm will not be responsible for training, and will engage individuals on specific jobs for specified time periods. Payment need only be made on achievement of required objectives. Make sure you consult the tax office regarding the tax position of sub-contractors.

On the other hand, daily rates of pay for sub-contractors are likely to exceed those made to employees. Problems of motivation and discipline may also be experienced as sub-contractors are likely to be unfamiliar with the firm's operations and standards.

Encourage overtime working

The advantage of using this approach is that staff are, as with internal promotion and transfer, familiar with company practices. The company is also aware of the employee's strengths and weaknesses. It offers the employee the opportunity to increase his earnings and the opportunity to finish the job which increases individual motivation and pride in the job. A major disadvantage, however, is that if used for prolonged periods of time, the overtime periods become a norm, can therefore be expensive and can lead to an 'exhausted' workforce which may not be able to be flexible as more orders arrive or production rises during peak periods.

Part-replacement options

Hire part-time staff

Part-timers can be used to cover peaks of production. An employee who normally works less than 16 hours a week, will not be covered by various aspects of employment legislation, so management flexibility is increased and the administrative burden lightened. However, the part-timer could well be detached from communication and information channels, and the same amount of money and time is probably needed to train a part-timer as is needed for a full-timer.

Hire casual or temporary staff

Again, such staff can be used to cover peaks in production. However their legal position needs to be closely monitored, for example, regarding start and finish dates, extension of contracts and transference to permanent status.

Administrative arrangements for tax and National Insurance will be the same as for a permanent employee, and certain statutory payments may be required, for example, statutory sick pay, depending on length of service. The statement of contract of employment and offer letter should show clearly a start and finish date. The length of employment should be ideally less than two years. If longer, the employees may have a claim to the same rights as permanent employees. By stipulating a finish date, a *fixed-term contract* has been agreed.

Job sharing

An examination of jobs within the firm could point to the possibility of sharing them. Prospects for carrying this out will depend on the nature of the job, the persons employed, and the nature of the workload. Job sharing occurs when, for example, all aspects of one job are tackled by two or more people. Person A may work mornings, Person B afternoons, effectively sharing one full time job between two part-time employees.

Job sharing should develop the pool of expertise within the firm, and should enhance flexibility, both by providing the capacity to meet peaks and troughs in production and by providing cover for absence or leave. It should allow for experienced staff to be retrained following maternity and other leave periods with savings in recruitment and training.

The company may be exampt from certain legal and financial obligations, in relation to pension schemes and employment laws, if job sharers do not meet minimum hourly qualification thresholds. (see appropriate chapters)

The employment of job sharers will, at least initially, lead to increased recruitment and training activity, and will demand increased supervision and monitoring of performance, as well as extra administration particularly regarding the payroll.

What type of person do you need?

If, having considered the alternatives outlined in the previous section, you decide that you need a full-time person either to replace a full-time person that has left or to cope with increased workload, you should first consider what duties this individual will perform Remember that, when replacing a leaver you do not have to employ the new recruit to perform all the tasks of the previous employee.

You may wish to alter the duties slightly to reflect changes in your business needs. This list of duties or *job description* will help you form an idea of the type of person you will need to fill the vacancy. You should then list the criteria that an individual should be able to meet before being considered for the position. This list is often referred to as the *person specification*

The following examples of a job description and person specification will serve as a useful guide to you.

Job descriptions

In small firms, employees will probably be expected to work with considerable flexibility. Job descriptions should reflect this, and jobs should not be defined too narrowly. A 'catch all' statement may be included such as 'Any other duties should be performed as and when required'. Even so, it is as well to make the job description as accurate as possible should difficulties arise. In Fig. 2.1 you can see a specimen job description for you to adapt for your own uses.

Checking with the current job holder and supervisor ensures that you have not missed any duties and can act as a reminder to the current job holder of what he or she is expected to do. Note that the name of the employee never appears on the job description.

Job description

Section:	Sales
Job title:	Telephone salesperson
Reports to:	Sales Manager
Responsible for:	Nil

Purpose of job

To contribute towards the achievement of weekly sales targets.

Duties:

1. Assist in preparation of sales brief
2. Contact potential customers over telephone and undertake to sell product
3. Inform Sales Manager of interested customers at end of day
4. Match activity with targets at end of day. Pass record form to Sales Manager
5. Perform general administrative duties as and when required

Certification:

Job description prepared by:

Seen by job holder and agreed to be accurate	.... Signature	.... Date
Seen by supervisor and agreed to be accurate	.... Signature	.... Date

Fig. 2.1 A specimen job description

The pros and cons of a job description

+	–
Defines job parameters and shows employees and managers what is expected of them	Does not allow flexibility in all cases
Useful as an aid to recruitment	Increases demarcation
Useful as an aid to appraising staff	May cause problems for job evaluation structures
Useful as the basis of job evaluation for pay rates, etc.	

Person specifications

Person specifications can be based on the following grading systems. These can be adapted or simplified.

Seven-point plan

- Physical make up
- Attainments
- General intelligence
- Special aptitudes
- Interests
- Disposition
- Circumstances

Five-point plan

- Impact on others
- Qualifications/experience
- Innate abilities
- Motivation
- Adjustment

Figure 2.2 shows a specimen person specification.

The pros and cons of a person specification

+	–
Focusses mind on major criteria for individual job	May too narrowly define person for the job
Can be used as a guide for internal and external recruitment	If inaccurate and used as a recruitment tool, can cause problems
Aids manager in handling unsuitable internal applicants	Internal recruits may be ignored because they do not match person specification exactly

Person specification

Section:	Sales
Job title:	Telephone salesperson
1. Physical make-up	Articulate, forceful and pleasant speaker General good health
2. Attainments	Normally 5 GCSEs including English and Mathematics Previous experience of similar work desirable
3. General intelligence	Quick to respond Decisive Good memory
4. Special aptitudes	Good telephone manner Good with figures Able to work under pressure and to meet deadlines
5. Interests	Practical and social
6. Disposition	Extrovert Friendly Confident
7. Circumstances	Must be able to work occasional evenings and weekends

Fig. 2.2 A specimen person specification

How do you get people?

When the decision is made to recruit externally, it is necessary to consider appropriate sources. These will vary according to the type of position.

Word of mouth

+	–
Inexpensive A reliable recommendation limits the risk of getting a poor recruit Recruitment of friends or relations increases loyalty to the firm Tends to be less formal	May cause legal problems if certain people are excluded from applying on the grounds of race or sex (see Chapter 9) 'In crowds' can be formed. Good friends or relatives do not necessarily make good employees Informal approaches run the risk of being biased. This would demoralise internal applicants

Notice boards

+	–
Inexpensive Reaches a large pool of potential applicants Knowledge of opportunity should serve to motivate internal aspirants to promotion	Limits field of applicants to internal candidates (and to those seeing the notice) May be seen as 'part of the furniture' and ignored If notice is accessible only to one sex or race, it could be held to be discriminatory, e.g., notice board in men's changing rooms advertising foreperson position

Job Centres

+	–
Free service to all firms Provides access to local market Centre will take responsibility, if required, for parts of the recruitment process Access gained to a large network of applicants UK wide	Individuals provided by Job Centre may not closely match operational requirements Centre may not fully comprehend job to be filled Quality of applicants to Job Centre varies regionally

Private agencies/selection consultants

+	–
Possess considerable expertise in the recruitment field	Expensive. Fees range from 8% to 25% of recruit's first year's salary
Possess detailed knowledge of certain specialist occupations	May pressure employer to hire a particular applicant
Will remove the need for pre-selection activities	Heavy sales pressure may continue to be exerted after the firm has recruited
Will normally not charge unless the firm recruits via the agency	Often inflate salary quoted to increase fees obtained
Could provide refund if recruit leaves within a certain time period	

- Check an agency's reputation before engagement. It is a good idea to build up working relationships with a few agencies.
- Remember that agency fees are normally negotiable.
- Always agree on fee before seeing a candidate, to avoid confusion after you have seen your 'ideal' candidate.
- Try to ensure wage or salary level of the recruit is established in advance so that an individual who cannot be afforded is not interviewed.
- Check all provisions of any contract struck with the agency. In most cases, if an employee leaves you within a certain timespan, you will be entitled to a refund or part-refund of your money.

Schools/colleges/universities

+	–
Provides scope to train individuals 'from scratch' although some schools provide vocational training	May need a settling-in period from school to work
Certain government incentives are available to companies recruiting school leavers	Will not be appropriate for certain vacancies because of lack of job experience
Improves the local reputation of the employer	

Newspapers, journals, etc.

+	–
A wide potential market of applicants can be reached	Can be expensive, particularly national newspapers
Particular markets can be targetted	Expenditure is made without a guarantee of suitable responses
Generally less expensive than employment agencies	Time and money is expended in producing advertisement

A simple review should be carried out following external advertising. This may be done by establishing the number of responses received through a particular medium, taking into account the cost of placing the advertisement. Also, a knowledge of the specialist area covered by journals and the type of reader will be useful. Find out what journals and newspapers your current employees read. In most cases, however, local advertising is sufficient to attract candidates.

How should an advertisement be drawn up?

Newspaper and journal advertising departments are usually helpful in explaining relevant costs and will advise on layout. It should nevertheless be remembered that their objective is to sell space, so the advertisement may not need to be quite as large as they suggest! Advertising space is also negotiable. You may have further grounds to negotiate if you already advertise in their business or trade section on a regular basis.

An effective advertisement will be concise, conveying the key aspects of the job, and it will stimulate a response. It should be drawn up carefully so as not to discriminate on grounds of race, sex or marital status. It should contain information on:

- the job title
- what the job involves
- the benefits of the job
- the location
- the type of person required
- the method of application.

If there is some uncertainty as to a suitable rate of pay, it would be advisable to exclude this information from the advertisement, and to request applicants to forward details quoting their current salary levels.

Administrators–Mortgage Department

Circa £8,500+bonus+benefits

Due to continuing expansion we now require a number of individuals to act as a back-up team to our field mortgage consultants.

As part of a small but friendly team the right person will need to show that they are dependable, precise and systematic in their approach to the job. In return we will be able to offer job security, a conflict-free environment and the benefits associated with a growing company.

Experience within the mortgage field would be an advantage, but is not entirely necessary as full training will be given.

Please write in confidence to:

(Name)

(Address)

or telephone me on (No agencies)

SALES PROFESSIONAL

circa £10 – 18K

We are looking for a special type of person. You are a self starter with drive and a competitive edge.

You want power to influence your own earnings. You want unlimited earnings potential. You want to take an active part in the progression of a growing multi-site agency. You want to be listened to and have your work rewarded and recognized. You want to work in a friendly environment where people are very important, and the work is constantly challenging.

We want to be able to offer you that.

Please write to me, enclosing a CV or telephone me for an informal chat.

(Name)

(Address)

Telephone number (No agencies)

Fig. 2.3 Two specimen recruitment advertisements

However, from experience, responses are normally higher if a salary level or approximate level is quoted.

Think carefully about the type of person to be attracted when writing the advertisement. The words used can be very important. Salespeople generally want to be in charge of their own destiny, and like unlimited earnings and freedom. Administrators generally prefer a stable environment, job security and a conflict-free environment. The examples shown in Fig. 2.3, when used recently in recruitment, generated large responses.

How do you choose the right person?

Assuming the vacancy is not filled by word of mouth, the next stage in the process will be to *screen* applications.

How do people apply?

Applications may be made in a number of ways.

By letter

Informal, and reduces the administrative burden on the firm, but the applicant is free to include whatever he or she likes

By curriculum vitae (CV)

A more extensive information checklist relating to the individual's experience and personal characteristics which is again drawn up by the candidate. It will normally include information on:

- basic personal details name, address, age, etc.
- work experience
- qualifications
- outside interests
- references.

By application form

Requires the applicant to provide personal information in key areas which are selected by the company. The receipt of a standard completed application form from all applicants will also facilitate the comparison of 'like with like'.

Occasionally, the requirement to complete an application form will deter a suitable applicant from proceeding with the application. Consequently, the firm should consider whether the information being requested is really relevant, given the nature of the vacancy. If not, less formal approaches should be considered. In any event, application forms should not be excessively complicated in format.

Application forms and CVs will provide useful material against which to structure the selection interview. Application forms of successful candidates should be kept as a useful record of personal information. Also, the forms of unsuccessful candidates should be maintained for a limited period (approximately three months) in case a selection decision is challenged.

By telephone

Encouraging telephone applications can cut out much of the 'red tape' associated with more formal selection mechanisms. The ease of application should encourage a large response, and the method provides scope for the firm to provide immediate feedback and information to the applicant. Clearly unsuitable candidates can be advised at this stage, cutting down the administrative burden on the firm. Of course, selectors should be very wary of making decisions about marginal candidates over the telephone as only a partial impression of the candidate can be gained in this way.

If this method is to be used, it is important that an individual who has major responsibility for the selection decision set aside adequate time to deal with calls following the placement of the advertisement. Candidates can be booked in straight away for interviews, bringing their CVs with them or filling out an application form when they arrive. If this approach is adopted a contact address and telephone number should be taken for the individual. This will help ensure that each candidate turns up and also means contact can be made if at a later date the interview time proves to be inconvenient.

Telephone screening forms are a useful tool when using this method. The example in Fig. 2.4. shows the basic questions that could be asked during the telephone conversation to provide consistency. This form can be adapted to suit any company and any position.

Separating the sheep from the goats

Whatever the method of application, the *person specification* is the key reference paper in the screening process as it systematically specifies the requirements for a suitable performer in the vacancy. Always compare the applicant's experience, qualifications and personal characteristics with those on the person specification for the job.

Secretarial

Name:	....	Tel no. Hm	....
Address:	....	Wk	....
....		Date of birth	....
....			

Where did you see advertisement? ....

How many years' secretarial experience do you have? ....

What equipment have you used? WP Electric Manual

How much WP VDU experience do you have (years)? ....

What do you think your current typing speeds are? 50 55 60 65+

Why do you want to change your present job? ....

....

Decision: Invite for interview Date/Time ....

Rejected on telephone ....

Rejected on CV ....

Fig. 2.4 A specimen telephone screening form

Telephone applications

If you are screening applicants by telephone, follow the procedure outlined below. If you are at all unsure, take the 'uncertain' route. You might end up with too many applicants, but it is better safe than sorry!

Decision		*Action*
Not suitable	⟶	Reject during conversation 'other applicants suit criteria more fully' Record reason for rejection in case challenged
Uncertain	⟶	Request further information (CV or application form)
Meets criteria (specified on person spec.)	⟶	Invite for interview. Arrange date and time immediately over phone

CVs and application forms

With these applications there is time for a more considered response. Remember, keep the person specification by your side. Follow the procedure outlined below.

Decision		*Action*
Sort forms into 3 groups		
Not Suitable	⟶	Acknowledgement Reject letter (see Fig. 2.5) Record reasons
Possible Candidate	⟶	Acknowledgement Delay reject/invite for interview letter. Place 'on hold'
Meets Criteria	⟶	Acknowledgement Invite for interview letter (see Fig. 2.6)

It is essential to ensure that you are selective, so that only a few candidates are invited for interview. Often 'rescreening' will be necessary between categories two and three, if there are not enough candidates matching up to established criteria candidates should be placed on hold for as short a period as possible, and informed of any decision immediately.

Reject on CV/Application form

Dear ....,

Thank you for sending me your completed application form/curriculum vitae recently.

After careful consideration, I regret to inform you that you have not been selected for interview on this occasion.

However, I thank you for the interest you have shown in .... and wish you success in securing a suitable position in the near future.

Yours sincerely,

Fig. 2.5 A specimen reject on receipt of cv/application form letter

During this process it will be useful to examine whether applicants could be considered for any other vacancies within the firm.

Simplified screening forms such as that in Fig. 2.7. overleaf may be attached to each application form on receipt as a summary document to assist in the screening and interviewing process. Additionally, the completion of such forms will establish whether advertisements are attracting suitable candidates.

The interview

As a small firm, you will be in a good position to run interviews on a relatively informal basis, and to combine the interview with a general chat.

Dear ....,

Thank you for your recent application for the post of .... I would very much like to discuss the vacancy with you further and have therefore arranged an interview for .... at .... to be held at the above address.

I should be grateful if you could confirm that this is convenient.

I look forward to meeting you.

Yours sincerely,

Fig. 2.6 A specimen invitation for interview letter

Criteria	Acceptable standard	
	Yes	No
Education	x	
Work experience	x	
Training	x	
Location/environment		x
Total	3	1

Fig. 2.7 A specimen CV/application form screener

In this way you can form a picture of the candidate as a person, and a view as to whether he or she will get on with prospective colleagues. In fact, prior to making your selection, you may wish to canvass informally the views of colleagues who may also have spoken to candidates.

It is essential, on the other hand, that some form of structured interview takes place so that the more objective criteria, such as experience and qualifications, can be discussed. The interview will probably be conducted by one or two interviewers, one of whom should be the direct supervisor of the candidate, should he or she be employed.

Try to avoid the known pitfalls of interviewing, in particular jumping to a decision in the first few minutes of the interview without fully considering the facts, or being completely swayed by factors such as the way the people look or the way they speak. If you adopt a controlled, informed and systematic approach, your interviews will prove fruitful. Remember that interviews have three main purposes.

- You can assess the candidate.
- The candidate can find out about your company.
- You can improve public relations. The candidate may be a future client or customer of your business.

A checklist for a successful interview

When you plan the interview:

- Ensure you and the interviewees know the time and venue of the interview.

- Ensure enough time is set aside for each interview (at least 3/4 hour).
- Read through the job description, person specification and application form and prepare some key questions in advance. If two interviewers are involved, subject areas may be divided.
- Decide who should conduct the interview. Individual interviewers probably possess the benefit of being more relaxed, however the individual may be more prone to bias.
- Set aside a room for the interview and arrange the seating on an informal basis. Avoid interruptions and distractions. Avoid telephone calls and people bursting into the room.

When you are carrying out the interview:

- Start by putting the candidate at ease by asking friendly questions, e.g. Did you find us all right? Would you like a coffee?
- Attempt to encourage an easy two-way and flowing conversation. Ask open-ended questions which encourage the candidate to volunteer information. For example, 'How do you feel about dealing with customers?' rather than 'You don't like working with the public do you?'. Questions that start with 'who', 'what', 'when', 'where', 'how', or 'tell me' will give you suitable answers.
- On occasions, probe or confront if he or she is being evasive or the issue is vague, for example, if there is a two year gap in a curriculum vitae. If the candidate is rambling, move on politely to the next area.
- Keep interviews as short as possible. Use time carefully and control the interview to ensure all key areas of the application are examined. Examine systematically:

  □ what the person does at the moment
  □ what the person has done in the past, previous jobs, schooling, etc.
  □ why the person is applying for this job, what his/her future plans are
  □ other interests, hobbies.

  For the prospective small business employee, particular attention should be given to social attributes, and the ability to work as part of a team should be investigated.
- You should *appear* interested in what the candidate is saying, and not act in a way that is obviously discouraging.
- Allow some time at the end of the interview for the interviewee to ask questions about the job. You should take this opportunity to explain the particular demands of employment in small firms, for example, the need to work flexibly.

At the end of each interview, you and any additional interviewers should record their judgements of the candidate, preferably against the criteria specified on the person specification. All candidates, whether successful or unsuccessful, should be informed of the outcome of the interview as soon as possible.

The usefulness of interviews may be increased if they are used in conjunction with other sources of information.

Selection tests

Aptitude and attainment tests are designed to predict the potential an individual has to perform a specific job or task within a job, for example, clerical, numerical or mechanical ability. All tests should be properly validated and run by experts. The Institute of Personnel Management provides training and information on selection testing.

Intelligence and personality tests are unlikely to be of much benefit to the small firm, and should be treated with caution. These usually have to be undertaken by trained specialists and can be costly and time-consuming.

Tips to consider when interviewing and selecting staff

(*a*) Make sure you are prepared before going into the interview.
(*b*) You may not necessarily like the person you are recruiting but that does not mean to say they can't do the job. The best person for the job may not necessarily be the one with whom you would go for a drink!
(*c*) Don't make up your mind in the first five minutes and spend the rest of the interview looking for ways to prove that you were right. Often first impressions can be wrong.
(*d*) Silence is a tool often not used by interviewers to its fullest. When you have asked a question which requires a long answer, you should then be silent. Looking at the candidate and nodding to them will encourage them to fill the gap and to speak.
(*e*) Remember, the more you talk the more the candidate will know about you and the less that you will know about him or her. The art of good interviewing is to get the candidate to talk all the time. Each time you hear yourself talking, shut up!
(*f*) Listen to the candidate and make notes. You cannot be expected to remember everything.
(*g*) At the end of the interview, explain to the candidate what happens next and make sure the candidate has no other questions that he or she would like to ask.
(*h*) Remember, if you are not sure once candidates have left you you can always invite them back again. If you are not sure after they have been

brought back a second time, it may well be an idea to follow the old proverb of recruiters, 'if in doubt, chuck them out'!

Second interviews

It may be that you have seen a number of people whom you like equally and you are therefore finding it difficult to decide. In these cases it is useful to bring back a short list of candidates to see again. Your impression of the person at the second interview may change your views and therefore help you to decide to which candidate you will offer the position.

It is also useful to introduce the applicant to the people that he or she will be working with. Normally this would be his direct supervisor or the person the applicant will be working with most closely. In a small firm it is particularly important that members of staff work together as a team and that there are limited personality clashes. You should therefore listen carefully to the views of your current workforce as to the suitability of an individual. Obviously the final decision will be yours.

Making an offer

Following the interview, it is advisable to earmark at least two suitable candidates for employment. This will provide a reserve choice should the preferred candidate decline the offer.

The offer letter

The initial offer can be made verbally, and followed up with the written offer which should contain information on the following:

- start date
- salary/wage and next review date
- hours of work
- holiday entitlement
- rotas (if applicable)
- grading structure
- fringe benefits.

A sample offer letter is shown in Fig. 2.8. In all cases, use probationary periods as a safety net for both you and the applicant to ensure that the correct decision has been made. As the offer letter will form part of the contract of employment, it is essential that all details are accurate.

Draft offer letter

Dear ....,

With reference to your recent interviews, I am pleased to confirm our offer of the position of .... (subject to satisfactory references) which will be based at ....

In this position you will be responsible to .... who will assign you your normal duties as discussed with you at the interview.

Your basic salary will be £ ..... pa and will be paid monthly/weekly in arrears. You will also be entitled to ..... in this position. Overtime is paid at the rate of £ ..... .

Your normal weekly hours are ..... excluding your lunch break of one hour. Daily hours are Monday to Friday/Saturday.

Your probationary period is for the first three months of employment after which time you performance will be reviewed and confirmation of employment made.

In addition to statutory holidays, your basic annual leave entitlement is four weeks. The current holiday year runs from ..... to ..... .

Full details of these and other terms and conditions of employment will be given to you on your first day and you should ensure that you keep yourself up to date with all items in the Company Reference Documents.

On your first day, please report to .... at ..... am. Please bring with you your P45 if you have one, National Insurance number and copies of your bank details.

I should be grateful if you could confirm as soon as possible acceptance of this offer.

I am sorry to have written such a formal letter. However, as you will appreciate it is important that we cover as many of the details of your employment as possible.

Finally, I would just like to add how pleased I am to be able to make this offer/that you have decided to join us and am sure that you will have a long and successful career with ....

I look forward to welcoming you on board on Monday ..... at ..... am.

Please do not hesitate to contact me directly, should you have any queries relating to this.

Yours sincerely

R Jones

Fig. 2.8 A specimen offer letter

Medicals

Requiring medicals can be an expensive business, so it is best to restrict this practice to jobs for which they are really necessary, e.g. those which involve driving.

References

References should be taken up to substantiate points such as:

- periods of employment
- type of work carried out
- periods of absence.

They should normally be taken from current employers, and should not be requested without the permission of the job applicant. They are usually taken up after the offer has been made.

If your offer is conditional on satisfactory references (as it usually is) or a medical, you should ensure that this is clearly stated in the offer letter, as it may be necessary for you to withdraw the offer if unfavourable references are received. However, it is advisable not to delay the applicant's starting date simply because a request for a reference has not been answered – referees do not always reply immediately! A quick telephone call is an effective way of getting a quick response. It is advisable to make a quick note of this.

Acceptance of offer

What happens next?

Once you have made your decision, and your offer has been accepted, you have entered into a contract with the employee, and a number of rights and duties, enforceable by law, arise. You should:

- Send out rejection letters (see Fig. 2.9).
- Arrange for a statement of the terms of the contract of employment to be drawn up. It is sensible to send two copies to the individual asking for one to be signed and returned to be retained on file. This statement has to be issued within 13 weeks of the date of joining and is usually signed after three months' satisfactory service. A sample of a statement

```
Reject after interview

Dear ..............,

Thank you for coming to see me recently with reference to
the position of ..............  After very careful
consideration, I regret to inform you that you have not been
successful on this occasion.

However I would thank you for the interest that you have
shown in ............... and wish you success in securing a
suitable position in the near future.

Yours sincerely,
```

Fig. 2.9 A specimen reject after interview letter

of contract of employment appears in Fig. 2.10 and a sample of a self-employed statement of contract is shown in Fig. 2.11.
- Arrange for the induction of the new member of staff. Someone should be asked to make sure that the new person is introduced to all employees and made familiar with the business in his or her first days. See Chapter 3.
- If you have identified any training needs during the recruitment process, you'd better start planning how you are going to meet those needs.

At the end of the day, the measure of a good recruitment programme is successful job performance. It's always useful to keep an eye on how effective each selection decision turns out to be, so that any weaknesses in your system can be resolved.

Action checklist

- Make sure you plan your recruitment carefully. Consider some of the cost-effective alternatives to full replacement.
- Draw up a job description and person specification.
- Decide how you are going to advertise the position. Draw up a concise and informative advertisement.
- Screen applications on the basis of the person specification.
- Interview short-listed candidates. Interviews should be well organised and encourage two-way communication.
- Draw up a statement of contract of employment and induction arrangements for the successful candidate.
- Send reject letters to unsuccessful candidates as quickly as possible.

Statement of Terms of Employment

In accordance with the Employment Protection (Consolidation) Act 1978 and subsequent amendments.

The following ia as statement of basic terms and conditions of employment between:

THE EMPLOYER:	.... and
THE EMPLOYEE:	Mr/Mrs/Ms/Miss ....
JOB TITLE:	.... at ....
REPORTING TO:	....
EMPLOYMENT COMMENCED:	Present job: .... Continuous employment: ....
REMUNERATION: (or as applicable)	Your starting salary is £ ..... pa Payment is made by monthly/weekly/ transfer on ..... Total pay and deductions are as on your itemized pay slip. Overtime is not usually paid in this position.
HOURS OF WORK: (or as applicable)	Basic ..... per week, excluding one hour lunch break. Normally from ..... am to ..... pm Monday to Friday/Saturday with a variable, rostered day off.
NOTICE PERIOD: (or as applicable)	From the Employer: 4 weeks From the Employee: 4 weeks
PENSION SCHEME: (or as applicable)	Your Employment is CONTRACTED IN to the State Scheme.

The following terms and conditions are detailed more fully in the COMPANY REFERENCE DOCUMENTS, which will be regularly updated. Copies are available on the Notice Board, or from your Manager:

HOLIDAY ENTITLEMENT AND HOLIDAY PAY; SICKNESS AND ABSENCE POLICY AND SICK PAY; GRIEVANCE AND APPEALS PROCEDURES; DISCIPLINARY RULES; NOTICE AND NOTICE PERIODS; OTHER IMPORTANT COMPANY CONDITIONS.

Any changes to these terms and conditions occurring after the date of issue of this statement will be notified to you within one month of such change, either in writing or by announcement on the main Notice Board.

I acknowledge receipt of a copy of this statement. I have read and I understand the terms and conditions of employment which I accept and I agree that these form the basis of my contract with the Company.

Signature ....

Date ....

Fig. 2.10 A specimen statement of terms of contract of employment

Contract for service

Between:

And:

Services

(a) The contractor will provide the services outline on the attached schedule.

(b) Any services provided other than those stated must be agreed by both parties and confirmed in writing by the Principal.

Fees

The fee for the total service is £4.25 per hour worked, and the contract is for a minimum of 37.5 hours per week. It is recognized that the tax applicable on these fees is the contractor's personal responsibility and is in no way a liability to ....

Term

This contract has been agreed for a fixed term of one year from 1 June 1987 and will expire on 31 May 1988. At this time the contract will be reviewed.

Termination

Termination of the contract can only take place with either party giving one month's notice in writing of the intention to terminate the contract earlier than the fixed period. The employer (...............) reserves the right to terminate the contract without notice if it is considered that the standard of work is not satisfactory.

Variation

No variation is valid unless confirmed by the employer in writing. If circumstances require, the employer reserves the right to vary the contract at any time. In those circumstances variations should be mutually agreed.

Undertakings

The contractor agrees to the following undertakings:

* non-disclosure of confidential information

* to abide by rules and procedures of .... whilst on company premises.

Signed for and on behalf of .... Date ....

Signed for and on behalf of the Contractor ...... Date ....

Fig. 2.11 A specimen self-employment contract

3 Setting standards and helping people achieve them

Helping the new employee to settle in □ Reviewing probationary periods □ Appraising employees' performance □ Approaching staff training

3

Helping the new employee to settle in

A depressing fact of life is that a large number of new recruits leave within the first few months of their employment. This can be due to a number of factors:

- failing to 'fit in' with the people they work with
- resenting management style
- having false expectations built up during recruitment
- being uncertain as to duties and standards required.

If someone leaves your business prematurely, you will have wasted all the time and money invested in the recruitment exercise, and the individual, too, could be adversely affected in future job applications as periods of short service are often frowned upon.

If you take the following steps, you might be able to prevent this happening.

Before commencement

- Inform all staff of the imminent arrival of a new member of staff.
- Allocate desk/work area/locker as necessary.
- Ensure that previous employees's desk/locker has been cleared and rubbish disposed of.
- Order essential work equipment or clothing, e.g. uniforms, overalls, protective goggles.

In the first few days

Primary responsibility for induction should be taken by the new recruit's immediate supervisor, who should:

- Explain the general activities of the firm.
- Introduce the new recruit to other workers/managers and explain how they fit into the overall 'picture'.
- Work through the job description, explaining standards required and areas of uncertainty.
- Ensure the employee is fully aware of working procedures and practices, e.g. Health and Safety rules.
- Ensure that employee is aware of factory/office layout, and knows where to find essential services/resources.
- Collect P45, National Insurance number and bank details for payroll, if appropriate.

Don't swamp the new employee with information on the first day. A 'softly-softly' approach to familiarising the new recruit with company practices should be taken.

After one week

Briefly review the week's work. If you identify any problem areas, attempt to rectify them quickly.

After one month

Briefly review the previous four weeks commenting on any obvious strengths and weaknesses.

After three months

Completely review the employee's performance. If continued employment is conditional on satisfactory completion of a probationary period, make decision at this stage.

Reviewing probationary period

After three months' employment, the supervisor or manager of the new employee will have a pretty good idea as to whether the individual is suitable or not. By referring to a simple set of criteria, the supervisor can establish whether or not the individual has successfully completed the probation period.

- Standard of work: quality and quantity.
- Personal standards: timekeeping and presentation.
- Ability to mix well with other employees.
- Interest in the job.

It is often useful to get the supervisor or manager of the individual on probation to complete a review form, usually after three months of employment (see Fig. 3.1). This helps the supervisor/manager collate his or her thoughts and impressions more clearly and encourages a more objective assessment.

Reviewing an employee once he or she has completed three months' service is leaving it a little bit late. You should have spoken a little earlier to discuss how the individual feels he or she is settling into the role. This also gives the individual some advance warning that he or she may be given notice after three months and time to make alternative arrangements. It will also help him or her to pinpoint areas for improvement and to make these improvements before the three months have elapsed.

If the employee's performance is not up to scratch, consider the following:

1. Has the employee been given adequate training?
2. Has the employee been told about his or her inability to perform?
3. Does the employee understand what is required?

If the answer to all of these questions is yes, then now is the time to consider giving the employee notice.

If the answer to question 1 is no, then you may wish to extend the probationary period to allow adequate training to take place. This decision rests with you. However, you should bear in mind the cost of recruiting a new employee may exceed by far the cost of training the existing employee. You should by now have some idea of whether this individual will suit the organisation. If you decide to extend the individual's probationary period this should be documented in a letter to the employee (see Fig. 3.2) and a copy should be placed on the personnel file.

If the answer to questions 2 and 3 is no, then this is your responsibility. As an employer, you have the responsibility to ensure your employees know what is expected of them and if they are not meeting requirements that you have laid down, they are given the opportunity to discuss this with you and also, importantly, the opportunity to improve.

Three-month review form

To: From:

Date:

To be completed by the direct supervisor of the employee.

Name of employee ....

Date of employment ....

Job position ....

Completing the first ..... months employment/Subject to re-assessment following unsatisfactory reports.

You should write your comments on all main aspects of job performance, indicating whether the employee is satisfactory or not. Give examples where you consider the employee is above or below average.

1. QUALITY OF WORK (Consider: job knowledge, technical competence, accuracy and/or thoroughness of work, neatness, telephone manner, etc.)

2. QUANTITY OF WORK (Consider: completion of duties on time, extra jobs tackled, speed of work, etc.)

3. CONDUCT AT WORK (Consider: punctuality, attendance, safety consciousness, care of property/equipment, etc.)

4. INTEREST IN WORK (Consider: attitude, adaptability, resourcefulness, etc.)

5. PERSONAL RELATIONS (Consider: attitude to colleagues, clients etc., relationships with other branches/offices, response to instruction/direction, use of tact, diplomacy, patience and self-control)

If there is insufficient space, please continue overleaf.

PTO

ADDITIONAL COMMENT:

PROPOSED ACTION:

These comments have/have not been discussed with the employee.

RECOMMENDATION
(Cross out whichever does not apply)

A. SATISFACTORY - Continue employment

B. UNSATISFACTORY - Review after ....

C. UNSATISFACTORY - Terminate employment

Signed .... Date ....

Fig. 3.1 A specimen three-month review form

Example of a letter extending an employee's probationary period

Dear Mr ....,

As discussed at our recent meeting there are still a few areas that you will need to work on before we are able to confirm your employment. At the end of the review period you should be able to (list areas of improvement required).

We have every confidence that you will be able to do this and have therefore agreed to extend your probationary period for a further two months and will review the situation again on ..... .

During this time we will continue your training and hope that you will feel free to discuss any aspects of the employment with us during this time.

Please do not hesitate to contact me directly should you have any queries relating to this.

Yours sincerely

R Jones
Director

Fig. 3.2 A specimen extension of probationary period letter

The following procedure is suggested.

- Review after one month. Talk to the individual, off the 'shop floor', in private.
- Review after two months. Talk again about progress and likelihood of confirmation of employment at the end of three months. Decide now whether to extend probationary period or give notice.
- Review after three months. Confirm employment or discuss progress in light of the extended probationary period as above.

Once you have made the decision, the following action plan will ensure that you follow the correct procedure.

Decision	*Action*
Satisfactory	Issue statement of terms of contract of employment and confirmation of employment letter (see Figs. 2.10 and 3.3)
Broadly satisfactory with a few problem areas	Issue statement of terms of contract of employment and confirmation of employment letter (see Figs. 2.10 and 3.3) Notify employee of weak areas
Unsatisfactory	Minimum period of notice. Follow up with letter (see Fig. 3.4)

Confirmation of Employment Letter

Dear ....,

We are pleased to confirm your employment with us following your satisfactory completion of the three month probationary period. I enclose two copies of your statement of terms and conditions of employment. Please could you sign one copy and return it to me as soon as possible.

As discussed, you will need to concentrate on the following areas over the next couple of months.

....

....

....

....

If you need any help in these areas, please do not hesitate to contact me.

I am pleased to be able to welcome you officially, and wish you a long and successful career with us.

Yours sincerely,

Fig. 3.3 A specimen confirmation of employment letter

Non-continuation of employment after three months

Dear ....,

With reference to our recent discussions I am writing to confirm the firm's decision not to take up your contract after your probationary period ends on ....

This letter serves to give you the official statutory notice period of one week. You will therefore leave on Friday, ...

Your P45 and final salary cheque will be forwarded to your home address. Could you please arrange to leave your locker key, overalls and any other possessions of the firm with me on your last day?

I am sorry that this particular appointment has not worked out, however I wish you success in securing a suitable position in the near future.

Yours sincerely,

Fig. 3.4 A specimen non-continuation of employment letter (after probationary period)

Appraising employees' performance

Appraisal is a formal and systematic assessment of an employee's performance and is common practice in many large companies. The extent to which you will find it useful in your business will depend on its size and the relationship you have with your employees.

Remember, however, that when everyone is busy it is often easy to forget to remind employees that you feel they are working well or to point out weaknesses as you spot them. A regular appraisal procedure will motivate employees to do better by giving them knowledge of results, recognition of merits and the opportunity to discuss work with managers. The information gleaned from an appraisal will also help you when you are considering pay increases, possible promotions or transfers, training needs, and disciplinary problems.

Carrying out an appraisal interview

It is very important that the appraisal interview is seen as another ingredient in a continuing communication process. The interview should merely formalize, and investigate in greater depth, what is already known through a series of informal chats. Appraisals should also provide the opportunity for employees to convey to you their thoughts on the firm. This can provide you with a view of morale within the firm, and, where possible, you can take action to deal with individual or general problem areas.

You should conduct the interview on a strictly one-to-one basis, in private, away from the employee's workplace. It should last at least 45 minutes and should be an open and frank discussion between you and the employee. Each should take a share of speaking and listening to gain an understanding of the other's points of view.

There is no right way to carry out an appraisal interview, but if you follow these guidelines, you won't go far wrong.

Preparing for the interview

You should consider the points listed in the performance assessment record form in Fig. 3.5. This is the form you will complete once the interview has taken place. This will help you to consider the overall performance of the employee, the targets you agreed with that employee at the last review and the results the employee has achieved.

Set a time and date for the interview and notify the employee at least one week in advance. Make sure that you have allocated enough time for the interview and that you will be free of interruptions.

It is also of vital importance that the employee also collects his or her thoughts before the interview. You could ask the employee to consider the points listed in the employee's preparation for appraisal form shown in Fig. 3.6. You should hand the form to the employee at least a week before the interview. This will give you a useful starting point for discussion, i.e. how the employee sees him- or herself.

Carrying out the interview

The interview should deal with work-and career-related matters. You discuss results, performance and facts. Listen, do not lecture. Base the interview on the job description, the person specification and performance assessment record.

If an employee raises a personal problem and you feel this may have had a bearing on his or her performance at work, it would be quite in order to discuss that problem. You should not raise 'personal' defects unless you think these have a direct bearing on the individual's performance at work.

- Take the trouble to put the job holder at ease with fairly casual opening remarks and by restating the purpose of the meeting.

STRICTLY CONFIDENTIAL

Performance Assessment Record - Non Sales

PART 1

Name & initials: ....

Office: ....

Date of review: ....

Time in the position: ....

PART 2

Please assess the individual's work performance and tick relevant rating, commenting as appropriate.

The rating should be an accurate reflection of the performance achieved within the review period.

The explanations of the ratings are:

1. Outstanding - consistently high performance well above the general standard, providing a clearly superior contribution to the business and team effort. It is unlikely that more than 10 per cent of staff will fall into this category overall.
2. Above average - performance to a high stndard, showing marked ability in some skills.
3. More than satisfactory - performance to a standard generally above the required level.
4. Satisfactory - acceptable performance in all main duties, displays adequate judgement and generally carries out tasks to the standard required.
5. Unsatisfactory - performance is generally below level required. Action needed for improvement or training required.

NR No rating - this should be given to individuals where a rating is inappropriate, (e.g new starters) the reason should be given underneath. It should also be used where the reviewer has no evidence of the individuals performance in a specific area.

Signature

The review is not completed unless it is signed by the reviewer and the individual. Signing by the person being rated confirms that he or she has seen the comments on the form and has had the opportunity to discuss them with the reviewer. It does not necessarily imply agreement.

Fig. 3.5 A specimen performance assessment record

	1	2	3	4	5	NR	Comments
Job knowledge							
1. Technical knowledge of particular area of work							
Application of knowledge							
1. Ability to							
a. Meet dealines							
b. Work under pressure							
c. Follow instructions							
d. Organize/set priorities							
e. Ability to work unsupervised							
2. Accuracy							
3. Administration							
4. Creativity							
Communications							
1. Written							
2. Spoken							
Personal qualities							
1. Working relationships with other employees							
2. Judgement and decision making							
3. Drive and determination							
4. Use of initiative							
5. Adaptability							
6. Interest in job							
7. Punctuality and attendance							
8. Personal appearance							

PART 3

Summary narrative on performance

Strengths

Weaknesses

Suggestions for improvement

What, if any, further training is required?

What are the priorities for the following year?

Individual comments

Overall performance rate
(circle appropriate rating) 1 2 3 4 5 NR

Review completed by Signature .... Name ....

Date ....

Review seen by Signature .... Name ....

Date ....

Fig. 3.5 A specimen performance assessment record *(cont'd)*

Preparation for appraisal

It is the Company's policy to appraise the progress of staff at regular intervals and it is intended that this should be a two way conversation.

You will be appraised shortly and given below are a few points for your consideration, so that you may be prepared.

1. Do you thoroughly understand all aspects of your job?
2. Is there any part of your work where you feel you need additional information or training?
3. How would you improve your own performance?
4. Do you have any suggestions which would make your job more interesting?
5. Are you satisfied with your level of responsibility?
6. What are your strengths and do you have any special skills?
7. In which direction do you hope to progress?

Some people may wish to raise these and other matters, whilst others will feel that many of these points are not applicable.

Fig. 3.6 A specimen preparation for appraisal form

- Take brief notes of the points raised at the interview and explain to the employee why notes are being made.
- You may wish to start the interview by asking the job holder what successes he or she has achieved during the past year and which things he or she is least pleased with and why.
- Advise the employee as to what you think of his or her performance in general terms, taking account of the employee's comments.
- Recognize good work.
- Discuss areas which need improvement.
- You should also outline the employee's possible prospects within the firm.

At the end of the interview

As the interview is coming to an end, you should summarise the key points raised and consider the priority tasks for the coming period. You should agree all this with the employee and record all details. The record in Fig. 3.5 can be adapted to your needs. For example, if you wanted to have a record for sales staff, you could simply insert an additional section entitled sales ability.

Sales ability	1	2	3	4	5	NR
1. Level of average monthly sales						
2. Relationship with clients						
3. Standard of service						
4. Mortgage referrals, if applicable*						
5. Instructions/Valuations, if applicable*						
6. Priority setting						
7. Closing the sale						
8. Average number of monthly sales	....					

* These examples would be applicable to a small firm of estate agents. You would insert here some measures which are specific to the nature of your business.

In theory, if you have completed an appraisal form well, you should be able to block out the name of the individual concerned and still know to whom it refers.

Make sure you end the interview on a positive note so that the employee leaves the room aware of his or her past success and determined to improve for the future in weaker areas.

Approaching staff training

Training is frequently seen as a luxury in larger firms, let alone in their smaller counterparts. The problems facing small firms include:

- difficulty in releasing individuals from the job in hand
- difficulty in finding institutions to meet the specific demands of small firms
- lack of internal training resources and expertise.

The importance of training

Training is important for a number or reasons:

- to ensure that vital skills are retained within the firm even if a key figure leaves
- to ensure that standards of work are maintained or improved so that

profitability is maximized. The small firm is less able to carry a poor performer
- to improve managerial skills within the company, and thus contribute to improved employee motivation and productivity
- to build up a pool of skills within the firm, so that job flexibility and ability to cover for absent colleagues is improved, as well as receptiveness to new technology.

The cost of training

Possible costs associated with training include:

- physical — maintenance, heating, lighting, rates, cleaning
- equipment — telephone, typewriters/word processors, photocopiers, paper, videos, overheads, flip charts, etc.
- people — salary and time spent in training, consultants fees (if appropriate), loss of people from their jobs, travel expenses, accommodation.

A systematic approach to training

You will minimize expense if you plan well and choose your training methods with care.

If you take the following steps, your training programme should be effective.

- Identify training needs.
- Select training method.
- Evaluate training effectiveness.

How do you identify training needs?

It is important that you review each training need on its own merits, and not train for training's sake. Planned training for future needs is of vital importance to ensure the smooth running of the organisation. Consider the following:

Problem		Action
Senior secretary to retire in two years	⟶	Provide necessary training for 'earmarked' junior
Lack of computing expertise	⟶	Select extra individuals for computer training
Expansion into new product market	⟶	Overall staff training programme to be implemented

Individual training needs can also be identified in the following ways:

The selection interview	⟶	Failure to meet requirement(s) on person spec.		
Induction	⟶	Unfamiliarity with vital area of company practice		
Performance appraisal	⟶	Identification of area of weakness in past performance	⟶	TRAINING NEED
Informal conversation	⟶	Individual stresses a need for personal development		

Which method of training is appropriate?

Having identified an area in which an individual needs help by training, the next stage is to select an appropriate training method.

On-the-job training

This is an inexpensive and practical method of training which normally involves the trainee working with, or observing, the supervisor or a more experienced employee on the job.

The trainee may simply observe the experienced worker, in which case he or she will benefit from not being under pressure, but may quickly become bored. On the other hand the trainee may be asked to carry out the job while referring to the trainer for guidance. In many instances there is a combination of watch and try until the trainee is fully trained.

Care should be taken to ensure that the trainer does not resent extra responsibility, for example in a payment by results system in which production targets may be missed.

+	–
Inexpensive	Trainee may pick up 'bad habits' or unacceptable short cuts from trainer
Training easily applied to practical situation	Productivity of trainer may suffer
Trainee does not have to stop work	Trainee will gain only a partial view of the firm's operations
Trainee is placed in a live situation	

Internally designed programmes

Training programmes may be produced and operated by the firm itself, possibly involving the use of external trainers or consultants. Such programmes are particularly useful for technical training or for familiarizing staff with internal rules and procedures. They offer the advantages of instant feedback to trainees, high degree of practical applicability, and relative cheapness. Materials can be adopted for future use with minimal cost.

On the other hand, lack of training skills within the firm may lead to an amateurish approach and a lack of interest from potential trainees. If the firm is considering running a number of internal training courses it would be worth sending a member of staff on a training design course to ensure the firm's programmes will be well structured, varied and interesting.

+	–
Useful for technical training	May be a lack of training staff within firm
Useful for internal procedures training	Lack of interest from trainees, particularly if trainer is not perceived to be an expert
Instant feedback to trainees	Sometimes lack of detailed knowledge of subject
Tailored to requirements of the company	
Relatively cheap	

External training provision

There is a wide range of courses available at every level: from the inexpensive programmes run and sponsored by the Training Commission to those offered by highly specialist management consultants. No formal academic qualifications are required for most of the courses. It is possible, especially on the longer courses, that grants might be available to you or your employees.

Most of the courses take place in universities, polytechnics and colleges of further and higher education, although management consultants often have their own premises and lease out country homes and hotels for their residential courses.

Colleges are now becoming more flexible in their provision of courses for small businesses with regard to the content of programmes available, the length, the mode of attendance and the expense.

Training consultants can normally provide expert advice, tailored to meet the needs of your firm. They do tend to be rather expensive, however, and so you should check their fees and reputation before taking them on.

For advice regarding what is available in your area and how much it will cost, you should contact:

- your local university, polytechnic, college of further or higher education
- your local Chamber of Commerce
- your local Training Commission office
- your local enterprise agency

For advice regarding what is available for your industry, you should contact:

- your industrial training board
- your employers' and trade association

For general advice, you should contact:

- The Department of Education and Science (Pickup Scheme)
- The Small Firms Service (Department of Employment)
- Your national development agency or unit
- The British Institute of Management
- The Council for Small Industries in Rural Areas
- The Institute of Training and Development

+	–
Training provided by specialists	Could involve considerable expense
Training technology likely to be more sophisticated than for on-the-job training	Could be difficulties in applying material to the work situation
New perspectives and outside expertise can be brought to bear on firm's operations	Will involve time off work
Useful contacts can be developed	

Open learning/off-the-shelf packages

Open learning refers to a variety of materials available – written packages, audio and video cassettes, computer programmes and practical kits covering a comprehensive range of business-related subjects. These are of use for those who wish to learn more, but who are unable to attend a college-based course. Developments towards open learning offer great opportunities to small firms as expertly produced packages, with direct relevance to job performance are cheaply available without necessitating release from the place of work. The TC-funded Open Learning for Small Business centre was established in April 1986 to promote the idea of open learning in small firms. The Open University Business School and the Open College offer distance learning programmes as do many other colleges and business schools in both the public and private sectors. Advice can be obtained from sources listed in last section.

+	–
Cost effective – prepared packages tend to be cheaper	Some packages can be expensive (particularly visual and computer-based material)
Training can be fitted into work and domestic commitments	Requires considerable self-discipline and motivation. May lessen opportunity to interact with other trainees (although interactive exercises built into some programmes)
Brings outside expertise to bear on company practices	
Ease of administration on part of company	

cont'd

Allows trainee discretion in pacing the material, and scope for self-assessment	Some packages will not be relevant to the particular work situation and specific training needs
	There may be a tendency for trainees to drift from programme deadlines if their performance is not being monitored or supervised

The National Training Index

It will be necessary to shop around and to test the reputation of bodies offering 'off the shelf' packages. It could be advisable to join the National Training Index which offers members objective advice on the quality of training materials. This is an expensive option, however, if you do not use external training on a regular basis.

Choosing a training method: a checklist

1. Is the objective of training to introduce new ideas and approaches? Will it benefit individuals to have contact with other organizations?

   If *yes* ⟶ *External* training or *open learning*

2. Is the objective just to remind individuals of something they already know?

   If *yes* ⟶ *Internal* training

3. Is training to be provided as a reward? (Think carefully before using this route.)

   If *yes* ⟶ *External* training

4. Is the objective to solve an organizational problem, for example, non-cooperation of two sections, for which one or two individuals are mainly responsible?

   If *yes* ⟶ *Internal* training with an external trainer

5. Is the objective long-term career planning?

   If *yes* ⟶ *External* training or *open learning*

6. Is the objective to provide practical 'hands-on' as opposed to theoretical training?

   If *yes* ⟶ *Internal* training or *open learning*

7. Is the objective to ensure staff are complying with legislation?

   If *yes* ⟶ Both *internal* and *external* training should be considered

8. Is the objective to familiarise staff with new technology?

   If *yes* ⟶ Both *internal* and *external* training should be considered

How do you know training is effective?

It is important that you check the effectiveness of your training programme. If it is not producing the goods, you are wasting valuable resources and you will not achieve your objectives. Try the following.

Obtain trainee feedback

A trainee evaluation form (see Fig. 3.7) should be completed by each trainee immediately after every training session, whether internal or external.

The views of trainees on the value of a programme can be rather subjective and unreliable. An enjoyable programme is not necessarily a useful one. Individuals could even evaluate external programmes artificially highly as they could appreciate the prospect of further days away from work.

Training course evaluation forms do not as a rule identify the person making the comments. This allows the trainee to evaluate the training and trainers without the fear of retribution.

Request assessment by trainers

On performance of trainees throughout the course. Objective tests should be used to establish this. This information should be treated with caution, however. Trainees will become suspicious of training if it is seen as an assessment exercise.

Obtain assessment by supervisors

Of trainee's work performance immediately following the programme and then after a six-month interval to examine the longer term impact of the training. Performance appraisal will be a useful mechanism in carrying this out.

Training course appraisal form

JOB TITLE ....

COURSE TITLE ....

DATE OF COURSE ....

COMPANY/DEPARTMENT RUNNING COURSE ....

COURSE TUTOR ....

Please complete the following questionnaire within three days of attending the training course.

Please answer question 1 <u>before</u> you attend the course.

1. What do you expect to get from this course?

2. Were your prior expectations met? If not, could you explain why?

3. How can the course be improved?

4. Was the standard of tuition (please tick)
   Excellent? Good? Fairly Good? Disappointing? Unacceptable?

5. If the standard of tuition was either excellent or disappointing/unacceptable, please comment.

6. Was the tuition pitched at the right level? Please comment.

7. What was your overall impression of the course content?

8. Do you need to attend further training
   (a) In this area?
   (b) In any other areas?

9. Any additional comments:

10. Manager's comments:
    How has the participant benefitted from this course?

Manager's signature ....

Fig. 3.7 A specimen training course appraisal form

Monitor improvement in actual results

The usefulness of this criterion will depend very much on the nature of the job, the nature of the training and how directly results can be measured. For example, the impact of a typing skills course should be quite obvious on the proficiency of a typist, but the impact of a supervisory skills course for managers may be far less evident in terms of actual results.

Action checklist

- Establish a basic programme for introducing the new employee to co-workers and company practices. Ensure the 'induction' programme is spread out over a reasonable time scale.
- If appropriate, review probationary periods after three months and take relevant action.
- Establish a basic performance appraisal system to establish training needs, improve communications and identify promotion potential.
- Conduct appraisal interviews in a frank and open manner.
- Take a planned and systematic approach to staff training through
  (*a*) establishing individual or company training needs
  (*b*) choosing a cost effective training method
  (*c*) giving feedback on training.

4 Paying your staff

How much should you pay? □ How much can the business afford? □ How do you find out the current market rate? □ What do you have to pay? □ The agreed rate □ Statutory sick pay □ Statutory maternity pay □ Holiday pay □ What deduction do you make? □ Payment procedures □ Types of payment.

The payroll is one of the most complex areas of business administration. In a book of this length all we can offer is a general overview of what is involved. It is, however, important that you are aware of the detail and that you organise this area of your business properly. It is therefore essential that you obtain the following publications:

From your local DHSS office
An Employer's Guide to Statutory Sick Pay
An Employer's Guide to Statutory Maternity Pay

From your local tax office
An Employer's Guide to National Insurance
An Employer's Guide to PAYE

These will give you guidance on procedures, record-keeping, etc.

How much should you pay?

Pay has long been seen as a motivator to staff. Pay that is perceived to be too low can act as a strong demotivator because pay is seen as an indication of an employee's worth to the company. Managers therefore strive to achieve an even balance between these two extremes.

When deciding how much to pay employees, you should take the following factors into account:

- How much can the business afford?
- What is the current market rate for the position?
- Will you experience future competition for key members of staff?
- What is the current inflation rate?

- Are you about to increase individual skills through training and therefore increase their market worth?
- What are the comparative positions involved, status within the company, etc?
- Which benefits may also be included?

Care should be taken to ensure that you do not pay over the current market rate. This is often the temptation, with employers confessing 'I can't afford to lose him or her'. In this position it is easy to be emotionally blackmailed into paying staff much more than their true worth.

How much can the business afford?

This is the crucial consideration. There is no point in paying employees high salaries in order to keep them, if the financial position of the company will suffer as a result.

As the payroll is the greatest expense to many small businesses, especially those working in the service industries, it is important to keep salary levels under control.

How do you find out the current market rate?

You should check the following useful sources of information. The final decision as to what the pay will be, however, always comes back to you, the owner of the firm. Obviously, in some cases, this rate must be set with local trade unions. However, you should always have a rate in mind around which to negotiate.

Advertisements

By scanning advertisements in the local and national press and professional journals, you will be able to gain a rough idea of what competitors are paying. It is important to take into account the fact that the salary offered is not necessarily the salary that is agreed at the end of the day. Care should be taken when using this method of assessing the current market as the eyes are instinctively drawn to salary figures we expect or want to see.

Employment agencies

Employment agencies will often be helpful if asked for their opinion and some actually do their own market survey from time to time which they send to clients. Again, care should be taken as it is in the interest of the agencies to increase the salary levels quoted in their survey. Their earnings are normally a percentage of the basic salary on commencement of employment.

Inflation rate

Another useful guide is the rate of inflation. Current inflation rates can be obtained from your local library.

Employer organizations

It is also useful to consult people, such as the CBI and other employers' organizations, who will advise you of the average settlement rate at the present time and also the average salaries for your particular industry.

What do you have to pay?

It is your legal obligation to pay the following:

- Pay agreed at interview and in offer letter, subject to certain minimum pay agreements.
- Statutory sick pay.
- Statutory maternity pay.
- Agreed holiday pay.
- Guarantee payments.

We shall deal with these in turn.

The agreed rate

How much you pay an employee is determined in the first instance by your offer, either verbal, or in writing (the statement of terms of the contract of employment). Once you issue the statement of contract of employment to an employee or send an offer letter, they become legally binding and you are contracted to pay the salary specified. You should therefore ensure that when you issue offer letters and statements, the payment details are stated accurately. See Chap. 2.

Wages councils exist in some industries and minimum wages are in force. The main wages council areas have traditionally been retail distribution, road haulage, hairdressing and catering.

From 25 September 1986 no new wages councils may be set up. The Secretary of State can abolish wages councils by means of a statutory instrument, provided he has looked at the current level of remuneration in the industry and has consulted with the people affected in the organizations. In some instances, when a wages council is abolished, the workers may be brought under the protection of another which is already in operation.

As a result of the Wages Act 1986, all the current wage orders issued by wages councils are limited to setting:

- a single minimum hourly rate of pay for 'basic hours' up to a total amount per week
- a single minimum overtime rate of pay for work done in excess of basic hours
- a limit applying to the amounts which are deducted from workers' pay for living accommodation provided by the employer.

Remember that these provisions do not cover employees under the age of 21, and that the older-style wages council orders (made before 25 July 1986) which covered areas such as hours of work and holiday pay are no longer in force. Care should be taken, however, that employees who were employed when the wages order was in effect do not have any contractual rights made at that time.

If your employees are subject to a wages order, you should keep records to demonstrate that you are complying with the terms of the order. These records may be inspected by a wages inspector and should be retained for three years. Heavy fines are made by wages inspectors in instances where employers have not conformed with the wages orders. This can mean up to £400 for each offence and for more serious offences can result in fines up to £2,000 and/or imprisonment for up to three months. It is therefore very important that you check that there are no current wages orders in operation for the type of industry in which you work. A call to your senior wages inspector will help you ensure that you are complying with the orders under the Wages Act 1986. I have listed below areas in which there may be current wages orders.

Current wage orders

Aerated waters (gb)
Boot and shoe repair
Button manufacturing
Clothing manufacturing
Coffin furniture (all workers)
Cotton waste reclamation
Flack and hemp wages order
Fur
General waste reclamation
Hairdressing undertakings

Hat, cap and millinery
Lace finishing orders
Lace finishing (holiday) orders
Laundry
Licenced non-residential establishment
Licenced residential and restaurant
Linen and cotton hank, etc.
Made up textiles
Ostrich and fancy feathers, etc.
Pram and invalid carriage
Retail bespoke tailoring
Retail food and allied trades
Retail trade (non food)
Rope, twine and net
Sack and bag
Toy manufacturing
Unlicenced refreshment

These wages orders are payable for all time worked up to a maximum of 39 hours in any one week. You may agree a higher amount, of course.

Statutory sick pay

Statutory sick pay (SSP) was brought into effect by the Social Security and Housing Benefits Act 1982 and associated regulations. Under this Act employers take over the role of the State in certain circumstances of paying sick pay to their employees. This Act came into effect on 6 April 1983 and certain rules were laid down which determine which individual employees are eligible.

Period of incapacity to work

To be elibible for SSP, an individual must form *a period of incapacity of work* (PIW).

This cannot be formed unless an employee has been away from work for at least four consecutive days, whether these are working days or not. If an employee is unable to work because of the risk of infection to other employees, he or she may also be covered under the definition 'incapacity to work'. Any day of the week counts towards these four days.

For example, an employee who normally works Monday to Friday can form a PIW if he or she is absent from Thursday and is still sick on Sunday. Days only count towards the PIW if no work has been done on those days. If an employee comes in for part of a day and then goes home due to illness this does not count. These PIWs can be linked to form one period providing they are not separated by more than 56 days (including Saturdays and Sundays). These periods are called linked periods. Each PIW has to be at least four consecutive days.

Period of entitlement

When you have established that a period of incapacity for work exists, you should then determine whether the absence falls within a period of entitlement (POE). This period of entitlement begins on the first day that an employee is 'incapable of work' and finishes when an employee returns to work. The POE also finishes when the employee has had his maximum entitlement under the scheme of 28 weeks. You should note, however, that each new period of incapacity to work begins a new 28-week entitlement period provided it is not linked to the previous one, i.e. they are more than 56 days apart. In such instances, it is possible for an employee to continually have linked PIWs. When an employee's linked period of incapacity for work extends over three years, the period of entitlement ends. You are also not liable to continue paying an employee, if the employment is terminated. The period of entitlement will also end if an employee is detained in legal custody or he or she goes abroad to a non-EEC country. If a pregnant employee falls sick in the period of 18 weeks before her expected date of confinement, she enters a 'disqualifying period' and also ends her period of entitlement.

Excluded employees

Some employees will be excluded from SSP. Excluded employees are employees that fall into the following categories:

- employees over pensionable age
- employees on short-term contracts, e.g temporary or seasonal workers
- employees earning below the current statutory minimum wage
- employees who have recently received certain social security benefits
- employees on strike
- employees who have not yet started work for you
- employees who are sick within the 18-week qualifying period beginning the eleventh week before the expected date of confinement
- employees in legal custody
- employees falling sick outside EEC countries
- employees who have a leavers' certificate showing a gap of 56 days or less since the last statutory sick pay day of a completed 28-week period of entitlement.

If your employees are excluded by one of the above categories you have to issue them with an SPI (E) form which will inform them as to the reason why you have excluded them from SSP. These forms are available from your local DHSS office. Contact your DHSS office if you have any queries about this.

If an employee's entitlement comes to an end, he or she should be given an SS1 (T) form to transfer back to state liability. An easy way to

SSP self-certification form

Name

Address

I certify that I have been absent from work from ....

(first day of sickness) to .... (last day of sickness).

Reason for absence ....

Doctor consulted Yes/No

Name and address of doctor ....

....

Certificate enclosed Yes/No

You must provide a self certification certificate which you can obtain from your doctor for the first seven days of absence. After seven days the doctor will provide you with a doctors' certificate.

I confirm that to the best of my knowledge the above is true and complete.

Signed .... Name (block capitals) ....

Fig. 4.1 A specimen SSP self-certification form

remember this form is that the T signifies Transfer. A guide to the SSP forms is shown in Fig. 4.2.

Qualifying days

Statutory sick pay is only paid to employees for their qualifying days. Qualifying days are agreed between an employer and an employee and are normally days on which the employee works. This means that an employee who is a part-time worker on Mondays, Thursdays and Fridays, for instance, will not receive the full weekly rate. The qualifying days for this employee therefore are Monday, Thursday and Friday. Under the requirements of the Act, there must be at least one qualifying day in each week. For cases of statutory sick pay the week begins on Sunday. The first three qualifying days in any one period of incapacity are waiting days and are not paid. Two periods may be linked together if they are separated by no more than 56 calendar days from each other and each spell of sickness lasts four days or more.

Rates of payment

Payment is based on average weekly earnings, calculated in accordance with SSP regulations. The current rates of SSP are available from your local DHSS office.

You should pay SSP on the first day on which an employee would have normally been paid salary if not ill. Remember that statutory sick pay is treated as earnings and therefore will be liable for National Insurance contributions and to PAYE income tax, if appropriate, (see later in Chapter). If an employee leaves your firm, you must issue him or her with an SSP1 (L) form. If, during the eight weeks prior to leaving, an employee forms a PIW, statutory sick pay is payable for at least one week. These forms are also available from the local DHSS. These leaver statements should be treated very much like P45s (see Chap. 7).

Withholding SSP

You can withhold statutory sick pay if you believe an employee was not ill or if an employee fails to notify you of the reasons for absence as laid down by the requirements of your own business. If an employee is meant to ring in by 9.30 a.m. and fails to do so, you can withhold SSP.

You cannot however withhold SSP if an employee notifies you on the first qualifying day that he or she is sick or you require this notification on a printed form. You may not withold SSP from an individual for failure to notify you if you require this notification more than once in every seven-day period or if you have not notified the employee of the rules to be followed for notification.

If you withhold SSP, you must give a statement as to your reasons if requested to do so by the employee.

Reclaiming SSP

You can reclaim statutory sick pay through your National Insurance contributions. However, in order to do this, you must maintain absence records that can be inspected by a DHSS inspector. These records must satisfy the inspector that you have followed satisfactorily the rules of the scheme. You must also provide evidence of the employee's incapacity for work. In these instances employers normally introduce a self-certification procedure whereby the employee signs a form to say that he or she was

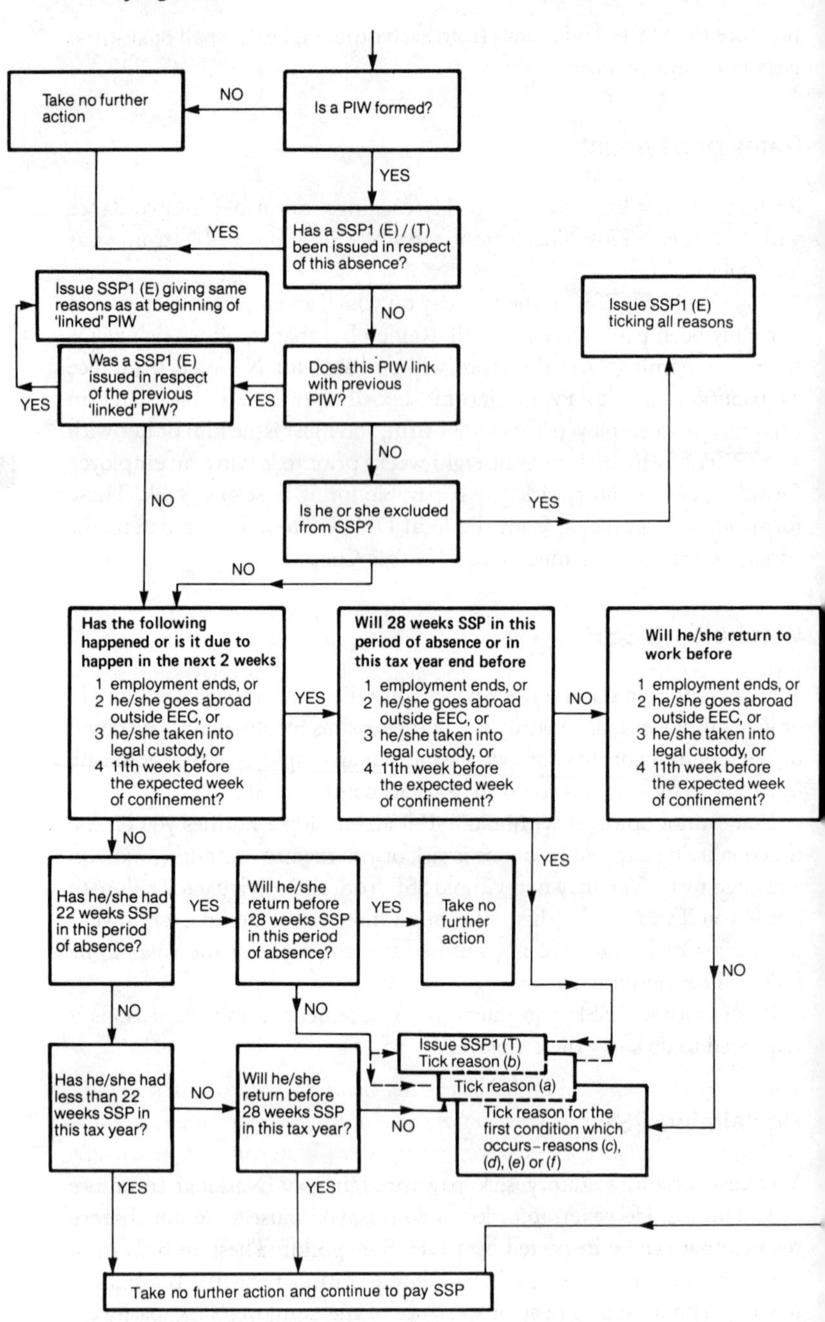

Fig. 4.2 A guide to SSP forms

sick on the specified days and is therefore claiming SSP. A sample form is shown in Fig. 4.1.

Penalties on employers

The Act poses penalties on employers for not complying with the provisions of the SSP scheme. The maximum penalty an employer may suffer is up to £2,000 fine and/or three months' imprisonment.

The details of the scheme are, as you can see, on first reading very complicated. You should therefore obtain a copy of the employers' guide to statutory sick pay from your local DHSS office to ensure that you are complying with the Act. Your local DHSS office will also help with any queries that you may have if you are unsure whether or not to pay an individual SSP.

Statutory maternity pay

Pregnant employees have certain rights: to time off, to maternity leave and to statutory maternity pay (SMP). Each of these rights is subject to different qualifying conditions. Employees are not necessarily entitled to all of these.

The rights

Time off

A pregnant woman is entitled to reasonable time off with pay during working hours to receive antenatal care providing she has a certificate of pregnancy and a valid appointment card.

Statutory maternity pay

From 6 April 1987 employees expecting babies due on or after 21 June 1987 who take maternity leave or whose employment terminates because of the pregnancy are entitled to receive statutory maternity pay paid by the company subject to their eligibility and certain qualifying conditions.

Statutory maternity pay is payable for a maximum of 18 weeks. This period is known as the maternity pay period. This cannot start before the eleventh week prior to the expected week of confinement (EWC). In order for an employee to receive the full 18 weeks'statutory maternity pay, payment must start no later than 6 weeks before the expected week of confinement.

SMP is paid only for weeks when the employee does not work for your company for any time.

Maternity leave

Some individuals will have the right to return to their former job or to a similar position at any time prior to the end of the 29 weeks after the date of confinement. This is known as maternity leave.

Who is eligible for SMP?

To be eligible for statutory maternity pay employees must have continuous employment (irrespective of hours worked) for at least 26 weeks by the end of the 15th week before the expected week of confinement (EWC). The 15th week is known as the qualifying week (QW). The employee must be employed during at least part of the qualifying week. The charts in Figs. 4.3 and 4.4 will help you understand the system.

The employee must also satisfy certain conditions.

- Her average earnings must not be less than the current lower earnings limit for payment of National Insurance contributions.
- The employee must stop working for the company wholly or partly because of pregnancy or confinement.
- Employment must continue to the eleventh week before the expected week of confinement or confinement must have occurred by then. Special provisions apply to stillbirths and confinements before the expected week of confinement.
- The employee must give written notice of the date she intends to start maternity absence or terminate her employment on grounds of pregnancy. This must be given at least 21 days before the absence is due to start. If less notice is given, the firm can decide whether or not it is reasonably practical for the employee to give the correct notice period. If the correct notice period is not given, SMP may be refused.
- Evidence of the expected date of confinement must be produced before statutory maternity pay can be paid. The doctor will normally issue a MAT B1 (maternity certificate). This evidence should be provided between the 27th week of the pregnancy and third week of the maternity pay period. The maternity pay period will be explained

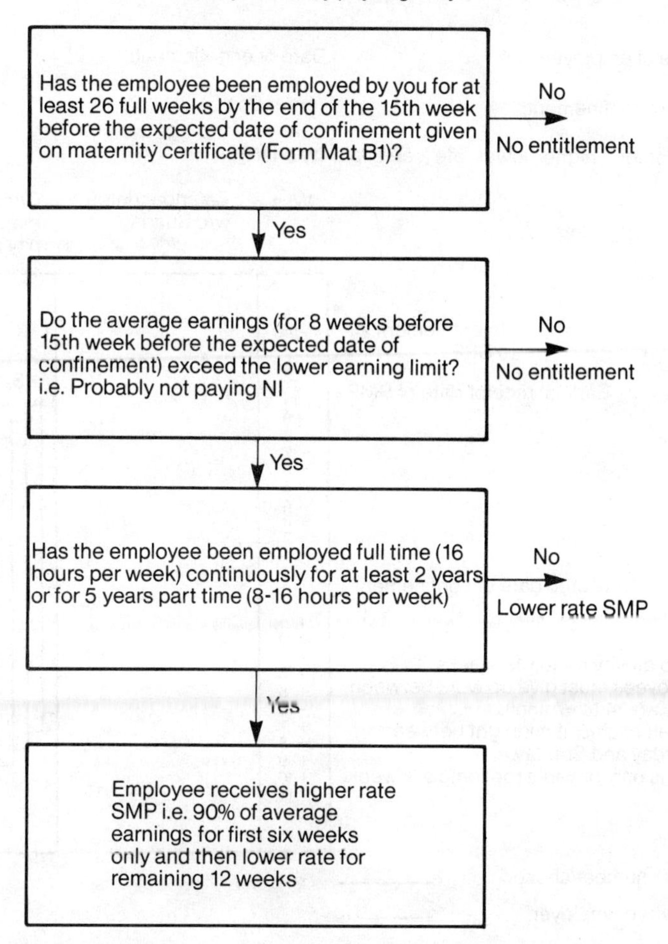

Fig. 4.3 SMP eligibility chart

overleaf. In exceptional circumstances only, this period may be extended for a limited time.

Excluded employees

There are certain individuals who will be excluded from statutory maternity pay. A woman will not be entitled to maternity pay if:

- She has not been employed continuously for 26 weeks.
- She is not employed by the company during the qualifying week.

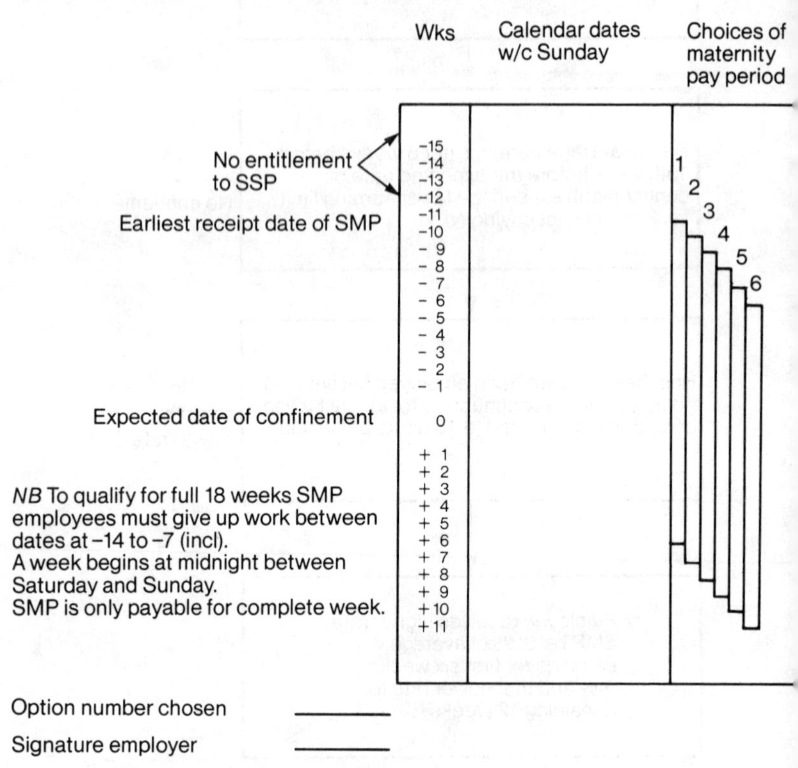

Fig. 4.4 SMP calculation chart

- Her average earnings are below the current lower earnings level (see *payment rates*).
- She does not notify her company correctly or produce written medical evidence that she is pregnant.
- She is abroad outside the European Community in the first week of the maternity pay period.
- She goes into legal custody in the first week of the maternity pay period.
- She works for another employer after the confinement and during the

maternity pay period and did not work for this employer during the qualifying week.

An employee who is not entitled to statutory maternity pay at the start of the maternity pay period does not become entitled to it later on. Obviously individuals should be referred to the state benefit system in these instances. You should complete an SMP1 form for any employee not entitled to SMP.

Payment rates

There are two rates of maternity pay.

The higher rate

To qualify for the higher rate, an employee must have worked 16 hours or more a week for at least two years. Employees who have worked between eight and 16 hours a week for five years will also qualify for the higher rate. It is calculated on nine tenths of the employee's average weekly earnings, based on the previous eight weeks. This is paid for six weeks. Employees then receive the lower rate for the remaining period

The lower rate

This lower rate of SMP is paid for 18 weeks to employees who are not eligible for the higher rate, and for up to twelve weeks for employees receiving the higher rate for the first six weeks. The amount of SMP payable is specified under the DHSS regulations.

Like SSP, SMP is subject to deductions for tax and National Insurance. Again, it should normally be paid on the day on which an individual would normally receive a salary.

At your discretion, you can decide to pay the SMP in a lump sum. However, this should be in exceptional circumstances only. If the employee loses her entitlement, you may find yourself in the situation where the employee owes you money. An individual who works for any part of the week during the maternity pay period is not entitled to statutory maternity pay for the whole of that week. You reclaim SMP through your National Insurance contributions, as you do for SSP. Again it is essential that you keep accurate records of each case.

Who is eligible for maternity leave?

To become entitled to maternity leave, an individual must be continuously employed by a company for at least 16 hours a week for not less than two years at the beginning of the eleventh week prior to the expected date of confinement. Again, employees who have worked between eight and 16 hours a week must have completed five years' continuous service before they become eligible. **Women who work in small companies employing under five staff do not have a legal right to return to work.**

Employees with qualified service who wish to leave their employment because of pregnancy are eligible for maternity leave providing they follow the correct procedures.

- Their resignation is in writing at least 21 days before the absence begins.
- The intention to return to work, if this is the case, must be specified in the resignation letter and a doctor's certificate showing the expected date of confinement must be produced.
- Employment must continue until eleven weeks before the birth unless the employee leaves for reasons related to pregnancy.
- At least 21 days' notice must be given of the intended date for return to work.
- The return to work should not be later than 20 weeks after the confinement date, except on confirmed medical grounds or at the request of the company. In these cases the return may be postponed for up to four weeks.
- Communication from the firm concerning the right to return to work must be acknowledged in writing within 14 days.

You can reserve the right to re-employ a person in a similar position, but not necessarily a position with the same content and terms of conditions as the position held previously by that person. Terms and conditions offered when the employee returns to work should not be less favourable than those that would have applied had the employee not been absent.

Where rights to benefits depend on length of service, the period of absence for maternity pay does not normally count towards the length of service. The period of employment before and after the break together constitute the total length of service. Entitlement to benefit is not earned during maternity leave and return benefits may be given pro rata to time worked.

Maternity leave does not break continuity of employment and counts as employment for notice rights, redundancy and further maternity leave.

To assist you in the correct calculation of the maternity leave period, the actual date of confinement should be notified to you in writing within ten days.

It is possible to continue paying a woman who is no longer in your employment. These employees will be employees who have no right to return to work. In these cases, you should discuss the situation with your local tax inspector.

For further information on statutory maternity pay, please refer to your local DHSS office and obtain a copy of the *Employer's Guide to Statutory Maternity Pay.*

Holiday pay

The Employment Protection (Consolidation) Act 1978 states that any terms and conditions relating to holidays including bank and public holidays and holiday pay must be included in the written statement which you give to your employee no later than 13 weeks after joining the firm. In most instances holiday and holiday pay will be agreed in the contract of employment.

An employee has no statutory right to paid holidays, except for:

- bank and public holidays (as agreed in the contract)
- young persons working in factories
- employees covered by a wages order made before 25 July 1986.

Guarantee payments

The Employment Protection (Consolidation) Act 1978 provides that employees with four weeks or more of continuous service are entitled to a guarantee payment up to a maximum sum, if they are not provided with work on a normal working day. The implications of this should be checked if this is likely to be a possibility in your business.

What do you deduct from pay?

All employees are covered under the provisions of the Wages Act 1986.

Normally the only deductions which an employer has the absolute right to make from the wages and salaries of employees are for National Insurance contributions and PAYE income tax. Under the Act, employers cannot make deductions other than these from a worker's salary unless:

- this was agreed in the employee's contract
- the employer has given written notice of his or her intention to make a deduction for a particular circumstance, and

- the employee has given written permission for the deduction to be made.

The Wages Act 1986 makes special provisions for employers in the retail trade: deductions can be made from the wages of retail workers, e.g. petrol station cashiers, for cash and stock shortages. Deductions are limited to ten per cent of the gross wage.

Tax

The limitations of this book mean that only the most important aspects of the tax system as it relates to your business can be covered. You should contact your local tax office and work closely with the people there. The tax office produces an information pack for those starting their own businesses. This is a very useful guide to setting up the systems so that your tax liabilities are handled properly.

It is an employer's responsibility to deduct the right amount of tax from employee's pay, keep a record of this pay and deductions and also pay the tax office the amount due each month. At the end of the tax year, an employer has to send a return to the tax office showing all payments and deductions made from individuals' pay throughout that year. The system whereby the tax office makes an employer responsible for the collection of taxes is called Pay As You Earn, or PAYE. All people who hold offices within your firm, including company directors are covered by PAYE.

It is important to distinguish between (*a*) those employed by you (in which case you are responsible for deducting tax from wages or salaries and paying it over to the Inland Revenue) and (*b*) those who are in fact self-employed but do carry out work for you (in which case the self-employed person is responsible for his or her own tax).

Employed or self-employed.

If you are unsure whether to treat someone as an employee or not, for example, for tax purposes, ask yourself whether the person can answer 'yes' to the following questions. If so, then he or she is probably an employee.

- Do you have to do the work that you have agreed to undertake yourself (that is, you are not allowed to send a substitute or hire other people to do it)?
- Can someone tell you what to do, and when and how to do it?
- Does someone provide you with holiday time, sick pay or a pension? (Though a lot of employees don't get any of these.)

- Are you paid so much an hour, a week, or a month? Can you get overtime pay? (Though many employees are paid by commission or on a piece-work basis.)
- Are you expected to work set hours, or a given number of hours a week or month?
- Do you work wholly or mainly for one business? (But remember that many employees work for more than one employer.)
- Are you expected to work at the premises of the person you are working for, or at a place or places they decide? (But remember that a self-employed person, such as a plumber, may by the nature of the job have to work at the premises of the person who engages him.)

If the person can answer 'yes' to the following questions, then he or she is probably self-employed.

- Are you ultimately responsible for how the business is run? Do you risk your own capital in the business? Are you responsible for bearing losses as well as taking profits?
- Do you yourself control what you do, whether you do it, how you do it, and when and where you do it? (Though many employees have considerable independence.)
- Do you provide the major items of equipment you need to do your job (not just the small tools which many employees provide for themselves)?
- Are you free to hire other people, on terms of your own choice, to do the work that you have agreed to undertake? (But remember that an employee may also be authorised to delegate work or to engage others on behalf of his employer.)
- Do you have to correct unsatisfactory work in your own time and at your own expense?

If a person is self-employed, he or she is responsible for:

- telling the local tax office that he or she is in business
- making a return of income to the tax office each year so that they can assess the tax due on it (the tax office will send a standard form for doing this)
- paying the tax: for the first tax year in which the person is in business he or she does not have to pay the tax until after the end of that year, but after that it is normally paid in two instalments, on 1 January and 1 July of each year.

If you are in any doubt, you should contact your local tax office who will advise you more fully.

You must operate PAYE even if an individual claims that he or she is self-employed or is a limited company, unless a tax exemption certificate is produced by the individual. In fact, you should operate PAYE if you are in doubt at all about any of the people working with or for you.

Tax rates

The tax rates are determined in the budget announced in April each year. The rate will vary according to the individual's level of earnings. The level of tax-free allowances will also vary according to the personal circumstances of the employee. Each employee is assigned a tax code which takes this into account. The tax office will supply you with a set of PAYE tax tables which will show you how to calculate how much tax should be deducted in each case. For more information, contact your local tax office.

For more information

You obtain help and information from your local tax office. Ask about the *Starter Pack* for new companies. You should take care, however, that the pack contains up-to-date information particularly if you are half way through a tax year. Other useful leaflets from the tax office include:

- Employer's guide to PAYE (P7)
- P8 cards
- Inland revenue income tax 480, notes on expenses, payments and benefits for directors and certain employees
- PAYE tax tables.

National Insurance

When applicable, you must deduct National Insurance from all employees'salaries or wages. A definition of an employee for these purposes is normally anyone who works in Great Britain with earnings which should be charged with Schedule E income tax. You will also have to pay an employer's contribution for National Insurance. If you are unsure as to your responsibilities, you should contact your local DHSS office.

Excluded employees

If your employee does not fall within one of the following groups of individuals, then both you and the employee have to pay contributions:

- employees under the age of 16
- employees reaching pensionable age (65 for men, 60 for women (this may alter in light of recent court cases))
- employees with more than one job, who give you an RD950 form
- some married women and widows who opt to pay reduced rates. This is now very rare as it has been discontinued and they must produce for you an exemption certificate CF383 or CF380A.

If you have an occupational pension scheme, you can apply for both your employees and yourself to pay contributions at a lower rate. This is known as 'contracting out' of the state pension scheme.

Payment rates

Employees pay different rates of National Insurance depending on their annual salary. They are broadly treated the same unless they fall into one of the categories previously mentioned or if they are directors of the company.

Company directors are not treated the same as other employees. If you pay either a salary or bonuses to a director, you should make sure you have an updated copy of form N135 and N1208 (bands of contributions).

The contribution that you pay as an employer will also vary as a percentage of the annual salary that you pay an employee.

You may claim back through your National Insurance contributions any payments that you have made under the Acts with regard to Statutory Sick Pay and Statutory Maternity Pay.

For further information

You should obtain a copy of the *Employer's Guide to National Insurance Contributions* from your local DHSS office. Other useful leaflets include non-contracted-out contributions CF391.

Attachment of Earnings Act 1971

Under this Act, an employee who has been ordered to pay a fine or debt by the court (applies to England and Wales only) may have an attachment of earnings order made on him or her. Under these circumstances the individual's employer makes the deductions from the employee's earnings and forwards them to the court. The employee's salary is still subject to the normal deductions for pensions, PAYE and National Insurance contributions.

These attachment orders are rare, but you should be aware of them. In Scotland, the Attachment of Earnings Act does not apply. Instead the Wages Arrestment Limitation (Scotland) Act 1870 limits the amount of money which can be 'arrested' from an employee's wages to one half of any surplus over £4 a week.

Payment procedures

Again there are no regulations covering how often you should pay your employees. This will be decided by you and the individual and will normally be contained in the contract of employment. You should therefore not change the pay date without consulting the employee or this could be construed as a breach of contract.

As of 1 January 1987, manual workers no longer have a right to be paid in 'the current coin of the realm', i.e. in cash. The method of payment of wages and salaries is agreed between employers and employees. In some situations, however, where employees joined the firm prior to 1 January 1987 when the Wages Act came into force, they may still have a right to be paid in cash.

Most firms find it more convenient to either pay by cheque or by a standing order to the bank. If you decide to pay by cheque, you should remember that employees will not be able to cash their money for three days after you have given them their cheque.

You must give employees on or before pay day, itemized statements of pay containing the following details:

- gross wages/salary
- net wages/salary
- variable deductions and the reasons for them, e.g. income tax, National Insurance
- fixed deductions and the reasons for them, e.g. voluntary deductions such as trade union subscriptions, savings schemes, etc., subject to the employees' written consent
- where different parts of the net sum are paid in different ways, the amount and method of each part-payment.

Types of payment

There are many different systems which can be used to reward staff. These include:

- time rates: hourly, weekly, monthly
- payment by results for individuals and groups of individuals
- profit sharing
- merit ratings
- rate for age structures.

Time rates, hourly, weekly and monthly

+	–
Set rate for the same individuals doing the same job	Does not reward individual effort
Ease of budgeting and forecasting salary bill	Does not provide an incentive to work harder than colleagues
Ease for payment for payroll purposes as standing orders can be set up and maintained	

Payment by results for individual and groups of individuals

+	–
Rewards individual and group efforts	Sometimes difficult to administer, time consuming
Increased incentive	Staff may appear in competition for payment by results on individual basis and therefore may effect working relationships
If group incentives, may create a strong team spirit	Budgeting for payroll expenditure may be difficult
Particularly useful for sales and production staff	Individuals in group incentive schemes may not pull weight
Gives employee authority in determining his own rate of pay and level of application	May not be appropriate to all staff, e.g. administrators

Profit sharing

+	–
Increases employee's feeling of participation in company. May be particularly useful in small firms Can be used for all categories of staff	Can be difficult to administer Difficult to differentiate on how much individuals will receive Does not necessarily increase productivity Erosion of profits as usually in addition to salary paid Employees in small firms in particular may speculate on total profits which may lead to dissatisfaction with their lot

Merit ratings

+	–
Rewards individuals for increased commitment and effort in particular jobs Discretionary Acts as a motivator	Needs careful handling to be perceived as fair Can lead to employees expecting merit payments as part of sales package if not paid on a one-off basis

Rates for age structure

+	–
Allows younger staff time to grow into role Allows staff to see salary progression	Individuals paid different rates for same job May not always be seen as a fair method of payment

Benefits

There are various other benefits that can be paid to staff in addition to salary. These benefits include:

- increased holidays
- sick pay scheme
- private hospital schemes
- company cars
- travel allowances
- pensions
- subsidised meals/travel
- subsidised purchases
- housing assistance.

The value of benefits to the small firm is usually in attracting and retaining employees. In all cases there is increased expenditure to the firm. Some benefits as discussed previously such as pensions are increasingly becoming accepted as the norm.

At the present time one of the main advantages of providing any of these benefits is that they often provide a benefit in kind which because of tax concessions is cheaper for the firm to award an employee that it would be for the employer to provide as part of the package offered. It therefore appears to be a greater benefit to the employee. It should be noted, however, that employees are taxed on some of these benefits. Consult your local tax office for details.

5 Managing staff

Managing the workforce □ Motivating the workforce □ Making mistakes □ Disciplining staff □ Coping with staff grievances □ Coping with staff absence □ Counselling staff □ Coping with stress

One of the major advantages small firms have over larger concerns is their lack of strict and formal management structures. When the firm is small, all employees and managers are often on first-name terms; employees are in many cases family, friends or close colleagues from previous jobs. There is a strong loyalty to the business and a uniform desire to see it do well.

As the firm grows, however, these relations will have to change. There will not always be time for an informal chat with each employee to make sure all is well and everyone is working hard. It may no longer be appropriate for the boss to be the employees' drinking chum and you will want to develop more management systems and a general management style of your own.

Managing the workforce

What management style should you adopt?

There is no one best management style and your choice will very much depend on the situation you find yourself in. There are two options: the 'you will' method and the 'will you' method. On some occasions you will feel it necessary to adopt the former approach, especially when you feel it is necessary to assert your authority. On other occasions, the 'will you' approach will be the most appropriate as you will be relying on the employees' full co-operation. It is important that you do not switch from one style to another too quickly.

What is the secret of good people management?

The secret of success is really to be yourself, admit when you are wrong and ask for help when you need it. It is an age-old myth that managers know everything. Staff may well know more than you and this can be very useful, if used properly.

To be able to manage people properly, you should always aim to meet the following five basic needs of the employee:

(*a*) Tell me what you expect of me.
(*b*) Give me the opportunity to perform.
(*c*) Give me guidance when I need it.
(*d*) Let me know how I am getting on.
(*e*) Reward me according to my contribution.

These five basic needs were defined by John Humble, one of the pioneers of management by objectives.

These needs are very obvious, but few managers ensure that all needs are satisfied for subordinates. A good manager will ensure that employees' needs are met in all of the above areas.

How do you approach decision making?

One of the most important functions of managers, and perhaps the function most often associated with them, is that of making decisions.

For newly appointed managers this is often one of their most difficult roles, as there is often fear of making an incorrect decision. It is obviously very difficult to define for any given situation a right and wrong answer, as this will depend on the number of variables present at that time. However, in order to make decision making more logical and structured a simple format can be followed.

- The first step is to identify the problem. If there is more than one problem present, try wherever possible to deal with one problem at a time.
- The second stage is to collect information that you may need in order to help you make this decision. This is particularly important when you do not feel you have the full picture of the situation. This information-gathering stage also gives you the opportunity to find supportive evidence for decisions you will make.
- The next stage is to look at the information you have presented and collected and look at the various alternative solutions that may be available. For each of these solutions, predict the effect this will have on the final outcome.
- The next stage is the decision making stage. You now have all the information available and have weighed up the pros and cons of the various courses of action you could take. Bearing all this in mind, you must now make your decision. Remember that at various stages we all make decisions which later on may appear wrong or out of line with

what we would have liked to have happened. However, by following a logical pattern there is less risk of this happening.

An important stage to remember and the stage most often forgotten or neglected is the collecting of information – stage 2. Many managers, when confronted with a question or query, feel under pressure to give an immediate answer. As a manager you should remember that you do not always have to make decisions at once. In business life, although many decisions are crucial, there are very few that have to have an immediate response.

There are various levels to this decision making process. Some decisions to which you will be able to give instant answers quite happily. However, never feel afraid to respond to direct questions by asking for some time to consider what has been put to you. If you tell the employee that you wish to have time to consider your decision and that you will get back to them, it is very important that you do get back to them to ensure that you are not labelled an 'I'll get back to you' manager.

Once you have made a decision, follow these four basic steps to make sure your decision is implemented properly.

Organize

The organization of the task is crucial to the final result. If this is not done the decision is often not implemented. Consider who is the best person or media to carry out the decision. This will depend on whether it is a task that needs to be completed or indeed a result which needs to be communicated.

Motivate

The next role of the manager in this process is to motivate members of staff to complete the task. This involves setting standards and targets, following up and ensuring that staff have performed their roles satisfactorily. Here responsibility is often delegated.

Liaise

You now act as a central information point communicating with members of your team collectively as well as individually. You will normally be the one person in the team who has full knowledge of the situation. You may delegate this responsibility again.

Control

You should review decisions on a regular basis, appraise them and adjust them in the light of changing circumstances.

How to make the most of your time

'... but I never seem to have any time ...'

This is probably the most familiar quote heard in large and small firms alike. Again, as for other problems, lack of time in a small firm is often more acute and the effects are more quickly felt than in larger firms.

Problems of time management occur in jobs where the amount of time spent in each area is discretionary, e.g. supervisory and management roles. The tools setter on a production line knows exactly what he is doing, how much he has to do and he will therefore set himself a pace to meet the target.

The supervisor and management roles by their very nature are changing constantly, although admittedly usually within guidelines (job descriptions) and therefore the day-to-day priorities change at the same time.

How often at the end of the day do you turn around as you are walking out of your office and suddenly remember something you should have done that day? Or someone reminds you that you said you would have something done by that date and you had forgotten?

It is essential that you make time for managing your employees, however. Often people management will be inextricably linked to the day-to-day management of the business, but you should also assign a certain amount at your time to purely personnel matters. This will show employees that you feel this is an important aspect of the business. If you show employees that you can manage your time properly, you will earn their respect and set a good example.

Draw up a To Do list

One of the ways to combat the problem is by the method called the *To Do list*. Many of us have one in our heads already, but being human we don't always remember everything on it or the priority order the items should follow. As with all great inventions the To Do list is very simple and straight forward and easy to use. Its effects are often dramatic.

You simply write down all the major things that you would realistically like to accomplish for the coming week. For example:

Find out about new telephone system
Talk to Jacobs *re*: American order
Place advertisements in next week's *Herald*
Management meeting
Check boiler in Unit 3
Calculate next month's target figures

Having completed your list, put next to each item the priority number indicating the order in which the tasks should be carried out. For example:

Order new machinery – 6
Find out about new telephone system – 7
Talk to Jacobs *re*: American order – 1
Place advertisements in next week's *Herald* – 2
Management meeting – 3
Check boiler in Unit 3 – 5
Calculate next month's targets – 4

Then simply work your way through the list updating where necessary and changing priority numbers as more messages are received that require action. For example, having spoken to Jacobs, the American order is going to be through next month and therefore you need to have the new machines sooner than you had originally anticipated.

Some items will be added to the list and some items may also have the same priority number. The main strength of the list is that you write down everything as it arises, assessing your priorities again by looking at the list and acting accordingly. It also means that you will not forget anything as it is already on the list. Be careful not to have too many items with the same priority number. If there are more than three with the same number, start again.

As with any system it takes practice. As your list grows, you can examine it to see whether what is on it needs to be done by yourself or whether you can delegate this to someone else to do (if you have someone to delegate to!). This is the part of the To Do list that as a manager of a small business you will find the hardest to do. Possibly in the beginning you did everything yourself and knew how well it was being done.

Once you have decided that some areas of the list can be done by someone else, tell them to do it, and let them get on with it. This doesn't mean that this item comes off your list but you simply put an initial next to the item of the person now responsible. You only cross off an item when you know that the person has completed the task and therefore your list can also be used as a follow-up tool. For example:

Bought new machine for Mitcham – 2
Find out about new telephone system – PAK
Place advertisement in next week's *Herald* – 2
Arrange management meeting – 4 – KA
Check boiler in Unit 3 – 5

If you encourage the use of the To Do list, by example, then you can also use the list as a method of finding out the immediate priorities of your subordinates. What are they doing? Are they missing something that should be on the list? Are they setting the right priority numbers by each item? You will be able to help them, letting them know what you as their manager feels should be a priority.

Moving on from the individual To Do list the next step is a Company To Do list. This will help you to forward plan the movements and events for your firm.

Set yourself a pattern

Another useful tool is to set out a pattern which can be used to effectively use your time, e.g. taking telephone calls from 9 – 11, making telephone calls from 2 – 3, signing expense claims and letters between 3.30 and 4. If you use this pattern every day, people will become used to it and will therefore plan their day around you.

Arrange your paperwork

Try to organize your desk so that you have a current file, a to do file and an out file. If you are not using a file during the day or have not touched it once during the day, it should not be in your immediate desk area. It can be stored elsewhere. We often clutter our desks and our files within our desks with information that we perhaps only use once a year.

Keep a diary

Your diary is probably your most important time management tool. If you have a secretary, you should always ensure that your diary matches the one that she keeps for you. If you are to follow up items in three months' time you can make a note in your diary on that day and therefore when you reach that day your memory is automatically jogged.

If you are going to hold a meeting with somebody, and you do not wish it to go on for a longer period than necessary (which it is prone to do), you could make the meeting before lunch. If you are running late for diary appointments, it is always better to say so. A short telephone call can often save much agony. If you have an important meeting to arrange or a diary date for which you need to prepare material you could mark this beforehand in the diary, i.e. three to four days previously.

Motivating the workforce

How do you get the most out of your employees?

To get the most out of your employees, they have to be motivated. There are a number of important points to remember when trying to motivate others.

Be motivated yourself

Probably the most important factor in motivating others is to be motivated yourself. Having an interest in the business and feeling part of the business and the business direction has motivated you. It may well be, by giving individual members of the firm a 'direction', a 'feeling' of involvement, you will motivate them.

You will be able to gain extra energy and motivation from your employees. The way to do this is to ask them for their ideas and be receptive to them. This will help them to feel involved and therefore become motivated.

Know your goals

If you do not know where you are going, you will never get there. People cannot work to their full potential unless they themselves have a goal.

Give employees goals

Younger employees or less experienced employees need shorter term goals than older employees. Three months when you are eighteen seems like a lifetime. Yearly targets or quotes are not motivational targets for most people. It would therefore be sensible to break them down into quarterly, monthly and weekly goals.

When people think they are close to their goal they will push even harder to get it. If the goal seems too far away it will act as a demotivator and they will not try to get it. Therefore, always try and make people's individual goals within their own reach. Show them how to get it, and show them how far away they are from achieving it.

Motivate from within

The goals of an individual may differ from the goals of an organization. However, individuals come to work to gain something, either within the firm or outside the firm. You should establish what this is. Once you have established what the person wants out of life, you can then point them in the right direction.

Although you will be able to motivate your employees to a certain extent much of this motivation has to eventually come from within them. A useful exercise is to ask your staff informally when they feel good (motivated) and when they feel bad (demotivated) while at work. This will help you understand what motivates them.

When they go home at night, if you would like them to recharge their batteries and be fully motivated the next day, one of the best methods is to win the family on to your side. If you motivate the spouse towards a goal, you also motivate the individual. To do this, you should include the spouse in the business at every opportunity. You could arrange sports and social events. These do not necessarily have to be subsidised by the firm to have the desired effect.

Acknowledge progress

People like to know how they are doing. Feedback is therefore very important.

Recognize the individual

People work harder for recognition than they do for money. However, it is true to say that if the money is wrong, i.e. too little, it will act as a demotivator. A 'well done' or 'good work' from the boss carries much more weight than the same amount of praise from a supervisor. Consider this case study.

Mrs Jennings works in the office from Mondays to Fridays from 9.30 a.m. to 5.00 p.m. with an hour for lunch. She is a reliable and hardworking individual who is always on time, always takes only half an hour for her lunch break and often works late to catch up on outstanding work. During the last two weeks she has worked even longer hours than usual as it is the financial year end. Everyone in the section is under extreme pressure. Mrs Jennings asks permission to leave early one Friday afternoon, her supervisor refuses, because it is the year end. On Thursday afternoon, Mrs Jennings' supervisor asks Mrs Jennings to stay until 7.00 p.m. as there is a major problem within the section. Mrs Jennings refuses.

What went wrong?

(*a*) There was no give and take. Mrs Jennings had spent years of giving and on the one occasion when she asked for a little back, it was refused.
(*b*) The supervisor did not ask Mrs Jennings' reasons for wanting to leave early and, knowing Mrs Jennings, it surely would have been something quite major if she asked to take time off?
(*c*) Mrs Jennings is now totally demotivated and will probably not want to be flexible herself again.

Although this might at first sight be an obvious case study (a common reaction by individuals is that 'I wouldn't do that') not giving and taking is probably the most common management error. It is also the most important management tool that you possess, that of 'give and take'. Organizations such as Marks & Spencer and IBM have founded their staffing policies on this philosophy and this is one of the main reasons for their success and good staff relations. As a small businessman, you can learn from their success. Remember, you only get back from staff what you put in.

Making mistakes

What are the most common mistakes managers make?

Trying to make popular decisions.

One of the most common mistakes that managers make is trying to be liked and popular rather than respected. This is primarily because everybody likes to be liked, and it is a very easy trap to fall into. There will be occasions when managers may have to make unpopular decisions.

Popularity is often short-lived. Our job is to be a good manager, not win a popularity contest.A decision should be made based on what is right for the business and if the decision also happens to be popular, then this can be a bonus. Making popular decisions that at the end of the day cripple the company will seriously threaten your popularity. Individuals expect you to do your job; doing it properly will gain you respect.

Giving favours

You should never accept a favour from a subordinate. Never ask subordinates to cover for you whilst you are not on company business. Never feel obligated towards an employee or overlook bad work as a personal favour. At the time it may seem like a good idea. However, you lose respect in the long run.

Having favourites

Never overlook faults, bad work, laziness or absenteeism as a favour, in order to be liked. This does not mean, however, that you cannot give favours to people outside of work or advice on personal matters. However always take care that your actions are 'seen to be fair'. Care should be taken when employing friends of supervisors who will come directly under their control, to avoid allegations of favouritism. Remember this can also work in reverse when friends are treated very harshly by supervisors, the friendship may be damaged as a result.

Discussing personal problems with subordinates

This again is a dangerous situation to allow yourself to be in. However, an explanation to individuals of why you are angry or out of sorts at certain times may sometimes be appropriate.

Sounding out about previous ability in the job

This is something we all tend to do. You were always the best advisor, the best man on site, the best junior accountant. Just remember how your previous bosses sounded when they went on about how good they were.

Socializing with staff

When we socialize with our staff, they see our weaknesses. This may not necessarily be a bad thing. However, this can often cause a conflict of interest between social relationships and job responsibilities.

Being disloyal

Sometimes young or newly promoted managers think they will create favour with subordinates by criticizing higher management, managers of a similar level or even their subordinates. This is not true. As managers, we should be loyal to our staff when required and be loyal to higher management when required. As a general rule, always be loyal to people further up the ladder than yourself. You will often find yourself 'sitting on the fence'. You should try to remain there as it is all too easy to be pulled in one direction only.

Failing to enforce discipline

Many managers also make the mistake of not enforcing discipline when somebody has acted outside what is normally considered acceptable. If the manager ignores it the employee knows he or she has got away with something. If the manager points out the lapse in discipline, the employee can be prepared for the consequences and will expect punishment.

Don't let somebody off the hook because you feel sorry for them. This is even more important when other members of the staff are aware of the situation. It therefore becomes more difficult to enforce discipline overall. If you are firm and fair you will get a reputation for fairness.

What form should the disciplinary procedure take?

A disciplinary procedure should lay down a series of consecutive steps.

1. For a minor problem ⟶ An oral warning
2. For continued minor problems or a more serious one ⟶ A written warning
3. For continued unacceptable behaviour ⟶ A final written warning specifying that if things don't improve, dismissal may follow
4. Insufficient improvement ⟶ Dismissal/suspension normally with notice (see Chap. 7)

Records should be kept of all written warnings, although provision may be made to 'wipe the slate clean' if conduct improves.

All disciplinary measures should be taken without delay, and based on adequate evidence. Explanation and information should always be given to the employee concerned.

To find out more about disciplinary procedures, look at the ACAS Code of Practice 1: *Disciplinary practice and procedures in employment*, available from HMSO bookshops. This area is also treated in more detail in Chapter 7.

Disciplining staff

It is important that a clear set of rules are drawn up so that staff know exactly what is expected of them in terms of conduct and performance (examples of each are given in Chap. 7), and what will happen if rules are broken. Rules should be:

- Fair, simple and specific.
- Applied consistently and immediately.
- Well communicated to those affected. All employees should possess, or have access to, disciplinary rules.

For further details and examples of disciplining staff should such rules be broken, please refer to Chap. 7 on dismissal.

Guidelines on disciplinary procedure

Oral warning

You should first talk to the individual concerned yourself, particularly if the evidence for poor performance has come from a supervisor or manager who works for you. Again you should take the employee away from the shop floor and talk to him or her on a one-to-one basis.

- You should ask some direct questions as to why they are not performing.
- You should not avoid the issue.
- Do not make the age-old mistake of going in firing full guns until you have heard what the employee has to say.

You should therefore always ask the question initially 'how do you feel you are getting on at work at the moment?'. This will give you some idea and indication of what the employee feels. If the employee feels that there is a problem he will readily want to talk to you about it. This may save you having to appear heavy-handed. If the employee has no idea that he is not performing well, this is the opportunity to talk to him about it.

You will be able to gauge how much has been taken in during talks with his supervisor or manager and whether in fact the manager or supervisor has been 'direct' when talking to the individual.

If we refer back to the disciplinary procedure, this would appear under stage one, first oral warning. You should agree areas of improvement with the individual, and set a time when you will review the situation. You should make sure that you give the employee a reasonable amount of time to improve. This may even involve retraining on certain issues. This should be done wherever possible and in more cases than not it is much more cost effective than recruiting and retraining a new person to the job.

Even if the individual has improved in the intervening period you should still keep the meeting. It is as important that the individual who has improved to have this improvement recognized as it is for the poor performer to have the opportunity of discussing why his performance has not improved in the specific period of time. The length of time that you give for the individual to improve will be very much dependent on the improvements needed.

First written warning

If at this second meeting there has been no evidence of improvement or only slight improvement you should again review the performance with the individual and explain the seriousness of the matter. You should again set a time period for the individual to improve and stress how important it is that the individual improves within this time. Again set a time and date for the meeting. At this stage you should follow up your meeting with a written letter to the employee, a copy of which should go on the

Dear ....,

I am writing to confirm the points made at our recent meeting and earlier discussions. As you are aware the firm expects certain standards of performance and unfortunately at the present time these are not being met.

We therefore agreed at our meeting that during the next two months you will make a concerted effort to improve in the following areas:

(List of areas that need to be improved upon here.)

I cannot stress strongly enough how important it is that you make every effort to improve your performance in these areas as failure to do so will be viewed very seriously by the firm.

I have every confidence that during the next two months you will be able to improve and obviously we will give you any guidance and assistance as necessary. You have recently been on retraining and hopefully this has helped you to review your job performance.

As discussed, we will meet again on 22 June 1987 at 10.30am.

Please, do not hesitate to contact me directly if you should have any queries relating to this.

Yours sincerely

R Jones
Director

Fig. 5.1 A specimen first written warning after a disciplinary interview

employee's personnel file (first written warning). (See specimen in Fig. 5.1.)

At this stage you should, wherever possible, avoid the phrase 'if you don't do it, you'll be sacked', although it is advisable to make it clear that failure to improve will have further consequences. This only adds to the stress the employee will already be feeling and will not help performance. You should, wherever possible, be supportive towards the employee. It is far more cost effective for the firm for the employee to improve performance than for you to terminate the contract and rehire and retrain a replacement.

Normally the first two steps of the disciplinary procedure will be enough to make the employee either improve performance or, if this is difficult or impossible, realise that it is now time to leave and look elsewhere. It is at this stage that an employee often resigns or looks for other work. Do not become complacent, however, and wait for an employee to resign. He or she may not and if you leave it too long, you will have to start the disciplinary procedure again from scratch.

Again the time and date for the individual to be seen again should be kept. If the employee has improved you should say so at this interview and give continued support and encouragement. You should explain how pleased that you are personally that the employee has improved and now settled into the job role competently. If the employee has made a dramatic improvement although has still not reached the standard it may well be that you give a further period in which to improve. At this interview if this is the case you should stress how pleased you are with performance to date and that you look forward in the next month or so to continued improvement to meet the standards required.

Final written warning

If there has been no improvement, you should discuss this with the employee at the meeting and set a further date and time for a further meeting. Explain that failure to improve performance, as discussed, before that date will result in termination of the contract of employment. You should follow this up with a final written warning (see specimen in Fig. 5.2).

If, after this final review period there has been an improvement, once again the meeting should take place and the employee's improvement noted.

If performance has not improved in the intervening period, you must terminate the employee's contract of employment. See Chapter 7 for guidance on where you go from here.

Dear ....,

Further to our recent meeting. I am writing to clarify the points discussed.

During the past ... months, you have failed to meet the standards required by the firm in the following area(s):

(Details of areas of improvement to be inserted here.)

As discussed at this meeting and at previous meetings, it is essential that your performance improves. We have agreed to extend the period of time in which you must reach the standards of performance expected of you to ....(date). Failure to reach and maintain these standards will, as discussed, result in termination of your contract of employment.

Please do not hesitate to contact me, should you have any queries relating to this.

Yours sincerely,

R Jones
Director

Fig. 5.2 A specimen final written warning after a disciplinary interview

How do you cope with absenteeism?

Recurring absence by an individual employee can cause major problems within a small firm. In essence you categorize absence into two areas: genuine and non-genuine. You must decide whether or not you believe an employee's absence to be genuine. Long-term absence requires a doctor's certificate anyway and therefore should normally be taken at face value.

In a small firm probably the best approach that you can take is the 'I am concerned for your welfare' approach. You will probably use this approach when an individual has had off odd days such as Fridays and Mondays and does not appear previously to have been ill. In these circumstances, you should take the employee to one side and talk to them about the recurring absences that they have had during the past few months. Ask them whether they feel that they are being given the correct doctor's treatment as you are concerned with the amount of absence that they have had. This then highlights to the employee that you have noticed the odd Fridays and Mondays.

If then the employee has been genuinely sick he or she will not feel desperately threatened. However, if the employee is malingering or demotivated into not coming into work, this could be your opportunity to discuss this.

It is best at this stage in the proceedings that you do not tell the employee that you do not believe the 'illness' is genuine. If after you have had this chat, there is no improvement in the sickness absence you should then see the employee again. You should ask whether a doctor has been consulted and if not, why not. You should also tell the employee that recurring absences are now becoming unacceptable to the firm and though initially sympathetic you now feel they are causing problems.

Obviously if the employee has been to the doctor you should take this into consideration as, again, the illness may be genuine. If the employee has not visited the doctor you should ask him or her to make sure this is done next time there are any signs of illness or next time he or she feels the need to take a day's absence. This should be done immediately on the first day's illness and the employee should ask the doctor for a private doctor's certificate for which you will reimburse the cost. This gets round the current system whereby an individual does not need a doctor's certificate for a week. This also deters individuals from having odd days off as they do have to go to the doctor. Again, this should be documented in writing and a copy put on the employee's personnel file (see specimen in Fig. 5.3).

If the individual is genuinely ill and this is causing a prolonged problem for you within the firm you are within your statutory rights to terminate

Dear ....,

With reference to our recent conversation I am writing to confirm the action that you will take in the event of further sickness from the firm.

Immediately on your first day of absence you will telephone me before 9.30 am. You should visit the doctor straight away and obtain a doctor's certificate. You may need to pay for this certificate and the firm will reimburse you, should this be the case.

You should keep me informed as to your progress as soon as possible.

Failure to follow these procedures will be viewed very seriously by the firm.

Please do not hesitate to contact me, should you have any queries relating to this.

Yours sincerely,

R Jones
Director

Fig. 5.3 A specimen letter confirming a request for a private doctor's certificate

the contract of employment. Under these circumstances you would need to ensure that you are able to prove that the employee has become unfit for the position for which he or she was contracted. It should be remembered that the longer a person is in employment the more difficult it is to establish lack of capability. For further information with regard to statutory sick pay and sickness rules and procedures within the firm, please refer to Chap. 4.

What should you do if an employee arrives late?

An age-old management problem is that of staff arriving late. There have been numerous excuses over the years to justify members of staff being late. Mostly these consist of train delays, local bus services and oversleeping. The occasional late arrival is not a major management problem. However, even if it is a one-off incident, it should be dealt with. If lateness is ignored it will recur more often. This can lead to individuals within the group accepting it as the norm and, therefore, instead of arriving at 9 a.m. every morning, employees will start drifting in from 9.15 a.m. to 9.30 a.m. The situation then gets out of hand.

Confronting employees with lateness is often difficult as it has happened to us all. The one-off incident therefore possibly can be ignored if an excuse is volunteered straight away. If no excuse is volunteered then you should investigate the situation and ask for the reasons why. This does not have to be a heavy-handed approach and it can be 'I noticed you were late this morning, is there a problem?'. This again is the 'I care about your welfare ' approach. The very fact that you have noticed the lateness is normally enough to stop recurrence. However, if it does recur without an acceptable excuse you have to sit down and talk to the employee about the problem. You should not ignore it. You should take the individual to one side and ask again whether there is a problem. If there is no particular problem, you should say that this is not acceptable to the firm and that you must see an improvement. You should also give a set period of time in which to improve. (Please refer to disciplinary procedures earlier in this section.)

Consider the following case study.

Mr Jones, supervisor, notices that Alex, one of the junior production workers, has returned from tea break five minutes late again. Mr Jones decides to ignore it. After all it is only five minutes and not a major problem. The following day Alex is again five minutes late. This continues for a week and Mr Jones continues to ignore it. As the week progresses Alex becomes later and later until he eventually returns from tea break half an hour late. By this time, Mr Jones has become more angry and decides to confront Alex in front of the other staff.

'Alex, you are half an hour late from tea. This is not acceptable and you will not do it again. I don't want to hear your excuses, you have been late every day this week, I've noticed. If this happens again, you are fired.'

Alex is extremely angry and embarrassed in front of his work colleagues. He has not had a tea break all week. His section has become behind in its paperwork and as they are under pressure to meet an important production deadline, Alex decided to do the paperwork during his tea break in the general office. Alex decides that he will no longer bother with the paperwork and as a result the deadline is not met.

What did Mr Jones do wrong?

(*a*) He should have confronted Alex in the beginning and asked him why he was late from tea on the first day he noticed it.
(*b*) He should have talked to Alex in private, again asking for an explanation rather than shouting at him. Remember, praise in public. Criticize in private.
(*c*) Mr Jones, as a supervisor, should have known about the paperwork problems.
(*d*) He assumed that Alex was at tea. *Remember* assume makes an ass out of you and me: *Ass/u/me*.

Coping with staff grievances

Just as an employer sometimes feels that they must take action against an employee, individual employees may sometimes feel that there is a need to complain about employer's actions as they affect them.

A grievance procedure should provide an open and fair way for employees to make known their complaints, to have these complaints considered by the company, and for the company to decide whether or not to accept or reject a complaint.

What form should a grievance procedure take?

A grievance procedure in a small firm should:

- be in writing (see Fig. 5.4)
- be known and understood by employees
- contain in general no more than two stages: the first stage should be raising the complaint with the foreman or supervisor and then if there is no agreement it should be raised with the employer. A grievance

Grievance and appeal procedure

If you have a complaint or problem relating to your employment, or if you are dissatisfied with any disciplinary action taken against you and you wish to appeal against it, you should take the following action:

1. Discuss the matter with the person you report to, if this is appropriate. This will usually be your supervisor or manager.
2. If the matter is not resolved satisfactorily, you should discuss it with the next person in line.
3. The final decision relating to any matters not included in these two stages rests with the Managing Director/Partner who should only be approached as a final stage in the procedure. At this stage you should put in writing your grievance and will receive a written reply, normally within 14 days of its receipt. Wherever possible, the matter and the stages through which it has progressed will be discussed with you prior to the final decision being made.

In order to help you present your case you may be accompanied by a working colleague at any stage in the proceedings.

In cases of appeal against disciplinary action the procedure should start at the level above that of the person who imposes the disciplinary measure, unless this is the person named at stage 3.

In cases of appeal against dismissal, and where employment would otherwise have been terminated, the employee will be considered as being on suspension without pay until a final decision is reached.

Appeals against disciplinary measures must be commenced within seven days of the relevant action.

Fig. 5.4 A specimen grievance and appeal procedure

procedure should allow the employee to be represented by a colleague in the second stage of the procedure if desired

Circumstances of each organization will affect the length of time taken to resolve the problem. However, most businesses should be able to complete both stages within 7 working days.

What type of issues are raised?

The type of issues that are often raised as grievances are:

- pay issues, such as bonus calculations and overtime entitlement
- holiday complaints concerning allocation of holiday period, etc.

- discretionary benefits such as paid time off for medical visits, unpaid leave of absence, etc.

How do you handle a grievance procedure?

- You need to know what the procedure is and how it fits in with your current policy and practice. You should ensure that all your staff in supervisory positions understand this procedure.
- You should listen attentively and evaluate what is said carefully by the employee.
- If somebody else is implicated you should listen to their story just as carefully and should not make any decisions until you have heard both sides of the story.
- You need to assess what has been put to you and decide whether or not it is a true grievance, a try-on or a plea for help. Some grievances may at first appear petty but may be hiding other grievances.
- You should reach a decision or verdict which is fair for the individual and business and consistent with what you hear. Be careful not to set a precedent.
- The decision should be communicated as soon as possible through all the parties who have an interest in it. You should also at this stage give any information on any appeal procedures which you may have within the firm.
- If, because of the grievance, there is an amendment to policy you should make sure that all staff are aware of the amendment.
- Always bear in mind that although grievances should be handled and dealt with quickly, you are able to spend time evaluating what you have heard from both sides and if necessary make a further investigation. Serious grievances may require a lot more thought, particularly if they implicate other individuals. Remember that reflection time is a very useful management tool.

Coping with staff absence

Staff absence can be crippling to a small business. In most cases the longest periods of staff absence will be their annual holidays. It is therefore essential that you plan these properly. As a general rule you should insist that employees agree their holiday dates with you before they book or pay for their holidays. You should adopt this policy wherever possible. There are many problems related to staff absence. These are discussed in the following sections.

Coping with halts in production

How do you cope if one member of the firm being away from work means that production has to stop?

If this is the case you may wish to consider specified holidays or a shut-down period, if you are not able to provide temporary cover. If you have not specified this in the contract of employment, you should seek everyone's agreement regarding the chosen shut-down week. However, it is not necessary for you to have everyone's agreement before doing this. You should consult unions if you are in a unionized environment. As a manager you have the prerogative to manage, and if you feel that this best suits your business then at the end of the day you do have the right to make these changes.

Coping during holiday periods

What happens if two or more members of the firm want the same holiday and you cannot cope with people being away at the same time?

You should talk to the people involved and explain the situation. It is often useful to do a first come first served policy for booking holidays. If you have not adopted this policy before the problem has arisen, and they have approached you at the same time, you could tell them that they should sort it out between themselves and once they have reached a decision as to who will be off at that time should let you know. Alternatively, if this will cause problems you should make the decision based on such factors as who has already had a holiday this year, seniority, length of service, etc. Remember to ensure you do not show any favouritism. If it is a particularly popular week of the year, you might suggest that one party has the week this year and one party next year.

Coping during peak periods

What happens if members of staff want holidays during a peak period?

You should adopt a policy that should be contained within their contracts of employment specifying that holidays cannot be taken between certain dates, e.g. in retailing the week before and after Christmas.

Establish the reason for their wanting the holiday then, and base your decision on that. Be careful not to set a precedent that others in future years may call upon as an example.

For instance, if a member of staff wants to go to visit relations in Australia and this is the only time of the year that is convenient, it may be reasonable to allow the time off as this will not recur every year. In these circumstances you should specify that this is an exception to the norm and ensure that this is documented. However, if members of staff have no particular reason for wanting to take annual holiday during peak periods then they may want to do this year in, year out. If you allow them to do this one year it will encourage others to follow suit in future years.

If a member of staff decides to go ahead and take the holiday anyway without your permission you will be entitled to discipline him or her.

What if an employee is sick while on holiday?

If a member of the firm returns to work after being on holiday, or telephones whilst on holiday, and says he or she has been sick during that time, first establish where the employee was on holiday as this will affect entitlement to statutory sick pay (SSP). For further details of SSP please refer to Chap. 4.

If the employee was on holiday outside the EEC, there will be no entitlement to SSP. The decision rests with you as to whether you feel you would like to grant additional holiday to the individual. The cost of this will be borne wholly by you, as you will not be able to pay or claim back SSP. The individual, however, may be entitled to social security and should investigate this.

If the employee was on holiday in this country or within the EEC countries, depending on the length of illness, an employee can be asked to produce a doctor's certificate to indicate that he or she was actually ill during that period. If a certificate is available, you will be able to pay SSP to the individual and therefore claim back the amount through your National Insurance contributions.

For instances of less than a week you can ask employees to produce a private doctor's certificate for which they will have to pay. You may wish to reimburse them for this.

The decision is therefore yours as to whether or not you wish to grant the employee additional holiday or approved absence. In these circumstances, the original holiday period could be transferred to sickness. There is no automatic right for the employee to claim more holiday in these circumstances. However, you may feel that it will reap rewards later on in terms of company loyalty and flexibility.

What if an employee asks for unpaid holiday?

Employees may ask for additional holiday. Under these circumstances, the time away from work is normally unpaid. The situation normally arises with new employees who have not accrued sufficient holiday entitlement during the current holiday year or employees who wish to travel long distances. You may wish to grant further holiday pay in special circumstances, e.g. to supervisors who have worked overtime all year and received no additional payment. Again, this decision is yours alone.

What if an employee asks for leave of absence?

Employees may wish for a variety of reasons to have some time away from work but eventually to return to work. Again this is normally unpaid absence. The reasons and lengths of absence must be discussed with you and then you can decide whether the request is reasonable or not. This normally depends on the individual's worth to the firm. You should gain assurances, however, that the individual will not work during his or her absence. It may be, for instance, that an individual wishes to set up his own business but would like the cushion of knowing that if things go wrong, he or she can return to the job with you. You should ensure that there is a start and finish date to the absence and that this has been agreed. Before granting leave of absence it is sensible to investigate the possibility of part-time working or even one-week-off and one-week-on, etc. see Fig. 5.5 for a sample letter.

It is sensible to put the reasons for the absence in the letter. This ensures that if later it is found that these reasons are false, then you would have evidence that could be used to dismiss the employee should you so wish.

Dear ....,

With reference to your recent request for leave of absence, I am pleased to confirm that the firm has agreed to grant you leave from 1 March 1987 to 1 May 1987, at which time the situation will be reviewed. We understand that the reason for this absence is to care for your mother who has recently undergone a major hip replacement operation.

This absence will be unpaid. Moreover, I must inform you that further absence may result in the firm having to terminate your contract of employment.

In granting this leave of absence, it was agreed that you will not undertake any paid work on your own behalf or for other individuals.

Finally, I would like to add on a more personal note that I wish your mother a speedy recovery. I am sure you will not hesitate to contact me should I be able to be of help.

Yours sincerely,

R Jones
Director

cc. Personnel file

Fig. 5.5 A specimen letter granting leave of absence

```
Dear ...............,

I was sorry to hear of your recent loss.  Obviously you must
take as much time as you feel necessary with your family.

I am sure tht you realize our thoughts are with you at this
sad time and that, should there be anything we can do to
assist you, you only need to ask.

Perhaps you could give me a ring in the next few days when
you feel up to it and let me know when you will be returning
to work in order that I can organize temporary cover.

On a personal note, please do not hesitate to contact me if
there is anything I can do.

Yours sincerely,


R Jones
Director
```

Fig. 5.6 A specimen bereavement message

What if someone requests funeral/bereavement absence?

Normally this is paid time. However, this may depend on the length of absence of the employee and in some cases the length of service of the employee. Although it may seem a little harsh to adopt a policy in this area, it does ensure that individuals who may abuse the system can be checked.

You may not know the person that has died personally. It will therefore not be appropriate to send a wreath. If you do decide to send a wreath, make sure that you have checked that this is acceptable to the family, for in many instances donations are preferred and in some religions, wreaths are not acceptable.

If you do not know the individual that has died it may be more appropriate to send a bereavement message to the employee (see specimen in Fig. 5.6). You can then arrange for the employee to ring in in due course. At this point you can discuss how much of the absence will be paid for by the firm. This is where it is useful to have a policy to which you can refer.

For example, you could say that when a member of the firm has suffered a bereavement, the firm will give paid time off in the following circumstances.

- Loss of a close relative (grandmother, grandfather, mother, father, sister, brother, son, daughter, husband, wife) – maximum two weeks.
- Loss of other relatives – maximum one week.

The amount of time allocated is at the discretion of the firm. Approved absence may also be granted in situations where it is felt necessary. This can be either paid or unpaid absence and again will be at the discretion of the firm. If employees are aware of this policy, it will make the task of arranging absence when a bereavement arises much easier.

How do you handle jury service?

Not everyone will be called upon to do jury service. However, when they are, individuals legally have to be released from work to attend. This can cause you major problems if the person is a key member of the firm.

Eventually the person will have to do the jury service. However, if it comes at a very disruptive time there is a possibility of postponing it to a more convenient time. In these instances, you should write to the clerk of the courts (see specimen letter in Fig. 5.7). Remember jury service can extend to several months and sometimes, in a major case, years. In some instances employees will suffer financial hardship if they do jury service. Employees in this category are often excused service altogether.

To the Jury Summoning Officer
The Crown Court

Dear Sir/Madam

Re: James Bloggs, number of summons 1.246/1

I am writing in support of James Bloggs' request to be excused from jury duty during February.

We are a small firm of chartered accountants. Many of our clients have 31 December as their year end and require their audits to be completed by the end of March. Thus we take on a significant amount of work during the months of February and March and all our staff are working long hours of overtime. James Bloggs has been assigned deputy leader of our audit team on one of our major clients and his existing knowledge of the client's affairs is essential to the smooth running of the audit. If it were necessary to replace him on this audit, it would cause further overtime to be worked as the new staff seek to acquire knowledge of the company.

In the circumstances, I should be extremely grateful if you could arrange for him to be excused from jury duty in this peak period of our business. If this is suitable, he will be available for jury service during the summer months when our work load is significantly reduced.

Yours sincerely,

E Smith

Fig. 5.7 A specimen letter requesting postponement of jury service

Payment to employees on jury service

If called upon for jury service in the crown court, high court or a county court, an employee can claim the following allowances:

- travelling allowance
- subsistence allowance
- financial loss allowance.

Please note there are no regulations stating whether or not an employer should pay a wage or salary to an employee on jury service. It is left entirely to the discretion of the employer. You should note, however, that the individual employee will be entitled to claim financial loss from the court if you decide not to pay his salary. It is important to note that an employee on jury service who does not receive any wages during that time is treated as being a non-employed person and would therefore need to pay voluntary National Insurance contributions to maintain a full contribution record. Further details of current allowances can be obtained on application to the court.

What if an employee commits a criminal offence?

Criminal offences committed by employees outside the work situation vary considerably. It will very much depend on the type of offence committed as to whether or not you feel that the employee should also be disciplined by you for this action.

Before deciding what action you should take, you should fully investigate the situation, wherever possible, to ensure that you have all of the available facts. Remember an employee is not guilty until proved so by the court.

If it is a serious offence the employee may well be held on remand. In these circumstances, it is often acceptable, if you should so wish, to terminate the employee's contract for failure to attend work. This decision again you can make in the light of the crime the individual is accused of.

Unfortunately, one of the most common occurrences with criminal offences outside work is that of drink driving. This is particularly important to you if a member of staff is employed as a driver. If he loses his licence you are therefore entitled to terminate his contract of employment.

Cases will vary from situation to situation. If you are in any doubt at all, it is advisable to contact a solicitor.

Once it is certain that an employee will be convicted, you may wish to send a letter in an attempt to reduce the sentence. A specimen letter is shown in Fig. 5.8. Often a solicitor representing an employee, particularly

Dear Sir/Madam

Re: Joe Bloggs

I am writing to ask the Court to take the following information into account when considering the case of Mr Joe Bloggs.

1. Mr Bloggs has been employed by the firm since 1 July 1985 and has always proved to be honest, reliable and trustworthy, so much so that Mr Bloggs has recently been considered for promotion. As it is an essential part of the new role for Mr Bloggs to be mobile he will therefore not earn the promotion if he is disqualified from driving.

2. It is also a condition of his current role that he must occasionally accompany clients to view premises. The firm recognizes the fact that Joe is a valued employee and will not be taking any disciplinary action on this occasion. However, the firm would have to review this position seriously if the situation were to continue for longer than twelve months. In the light of the above information we would ask the Court to consider this case favourably.

Yours sincerely,

R Jones
Director

Fig. 5.8 A specimen letter in support of a reduced sentence for a drink driving offence

if the employee is a driver of the firm, will ask you to write a similar letter in support of the employee to try to influence the court.

Counselling staff

How do you approach staff, if you suspect they have a problem?

You may feel the need to counsel staff yourself because a member of staff seems troubled or is off form.

If you are concerned about the behaviour of a member of your staff, you should deal with this in the following way.

- If you believe it to be a personal problem rather than a work related problem, unless it is affecting the individual's work – or indeed your help is sought by the individual concerned, as a rule of thumb you should leave well alone. You do not have the right to pry into an individual's personal life and indeed this can sometimes become dangerous.

If it is affecting the work of the individual you should have a quiet chat to the individual. Explain initially that you can see that the person concerned is not him or herself at work at the moment and ask if there is any way you can help solve the problem. Explain that it has now come to the stage that it is affecting work. It may be at this stage that you discover it is a work-related problem rather than a personal one.

Never tell an individual how to sort out his personal life. Your role in personal matters is entirely advisory. You can, however, make suggestions such as referring an individual to professionally qualified bodies, for example, marriage guidance counsellors or Alcoholics Anonymous. You are not qualified to sort out these types of problems and you should explain this to the individual and refer them to professional counsellors.

- If you suspect or know that an employee is concerned about a work-related problem, ask the individual how things are going at the moment and ask whether there are any problems. The answer will enable you to adjust your approach to the conversation. If the employee does not feel there are any problems, you will have to approach the subject more carefully than if he or she automatically pours out the problems and agrees with your perception of the situation wholeheartedly. You should explain to the individual how you see the problem and the way it is affecting the individual's performance at work. You should ask the individual for his or her perception of the problem, how it affects work and what can be done about the situation, either with your help or from the individual's point of view. You should then agree a course of action together and arrange a follow-up meeting to monitor any progress made. This future meeting should be set at this initial interview to ensure that follow-up will take place.

A check list

- Start by asking the individual whether there are any problems at work or at home at the moment.
- Explain your perception of the problem.
- Ask the individual how he or she perceives solving the problem.
- Explain how you feel the problem could be solved taking into account the individual's comments.
- Agree a solution/action plan.
- Set a time and date to review progress.

How do you handle staff who approach you about a problem?

Staff will often come to you seeking advice on both work-related and personal issues. When a member of staff approaches you to talk to you in confidence or asks for some advice, your main role at this meeting is to listen carefully to what is being said to you. In this way you will encourage individuals to become more frank and honest. Remember the problem that they initially discuss may not be the underlying problem.

You may have to create the right environment for the individual to be able to trust you. If you make comments too early, you may give the impression of being on the wrong side of the fence. You should therefore listen carefully to the individual and give him both verbal and non-verbal signs of encouragement. Listening is a skill that we all believe we are good at. However, like many other skills if it is not used often it will be lost. A good listener actively thinks about what is being said. A useful tool to encourage conversation and to also clarify what the individual has said is to repeat back to the individual what you believe he or she is saying. For example, 'So you believe that ...'.

Work-related problems

These are dealt with very much in the same way as if you had approached a member of staff. If it is a problem with a work colleague, it is better to let the individual sort it out for himself/herself rather than volunteering to 'have a word'. This usually only leads to further tension. There will be occasions, however, when you will have to use your discretion. Use the action plan in the previous section.

Personal problems

Here more than ever you should be a listening ear. Most individuals who discuss their personal problems with you do it for one of two reasons.

- They believe that it is now beginning to affect their work.
- They are using you as a sounding block to reflect their own thoughts.

Individuals often claim not to know what to do and will often ask you to help them decide. You should never be tempted by this. Your role is an advisory one and not a decision-making one. The decision must rest with the individual. More often than not in their own mind, they will have made a decision.

If there is no decision to be made a sympathetic ear is always appreciated.

A word of caution

Many individuals will become dependent on a counsellor if care is not taken to avoid this. You should watch for these signs and try if possible to direct staff away from you. Always be prepared to refer individuals to specialised counsellors. These people are trained to deal with areas of which you will have no knowledge. Through your ignorance you may cause more damage than help.

Coping with stress

How do you cope with stress?

Stress is a combination of demands made upon both our physical and mental energy. When this overload becomes to great, stress-related symptoms begin to emerge.

The first symptoms are normally irritability, excessive drinking, depressions, headaches, chest pains, raised blood pressure, and sometimes lack of interest in sex. These symptoms, if not checked, can lead to more serious stress-related illnesses such as coronary heart disease, mental illness and various forms of ulcer. You should keep an eye out for these symptoms in the members of your workforce and, of course, recognize them when you are showing them yourself.

Some individuals who are excessively competitive, have inbuilt feelings of responsibility and become completely involved in their work are more often than not susceptible to coronary heart attacks. Calmer individuals, who may often appear to cope on the surface, can also be prone to coronary heart disease.

Stress at work can occur at the following times:

- When there is too much or too little work. Both will eventually have the same effect.
- Where there is a lack of understanding of the individual and what he is expected to do.
- Where there is a lack of capability for the individual to perform in a certain role that is expected of him.
- Where an individual reports to more than one person directly or there is discretion in the job role in setting priorities, e.g., supervisory roles.
- Where individuals have to make decisions that will affect other people at work.
- Where career prospects appear limited or conversely when an individual is expected to want career progression when in fact he or she does not feel capable or able, or in some cases does not want it.
- Where there are poor working relationships with colleagues.
- Where the balance between working life and home life is affected and an individual is torn between the two roles.

Strategies for dealing with stress

- Identify the source or sources of stress.
- Attempt to reduce or eliminate the source. Can someone else do part of the role? Go home. Talk to individuals who may be causing stress at work. Try to ascertain the route of conflict.
- Set aside half an hour per day to do something unstressful, e.g. listening to music, painting. This will allow your body to relax.
- Physical exercise will reduce the adrenalin that is produced by a body that is under stress. Take up some form of sport. Remember to do this gently at first and don't push yourself too far. If you don't enjoy it, this will only increase the stress. However, after the first few weeks you will find that you enjoy the exercise and that you cope better with stress as a result of it.
- Try to take a holiday or, if this is not possible, a weekend break.
- Reduce your intake of alcohol and cigarettes.
- Reduce your intake of fatty and high cholesterol foods. Eat less red meat. This in itself will not reduce the stress but will ensure that the body is in a fitter state to cope with the stress.
- Reduce your intake of coffee or switch to a decaffeinated brand. Caffeine in coffee raises the heart beat quite considerably and so increases the symptoms associated with stress.

If you know one of your employees is suffering from stress, you should discuss the problem with him and suggest some of the above measures. If you do not confront the issue, the situation will only get worse.

6 Employee relations

Why is consultation important? □ What communication methods should be used? □ What is a trade union? □ Trade unions and the small business □ Handling trade unions □ The closed shop □ Guidelines for employee representation □ What are the rights of recognized trade unions? □ What are the rights of trade union members? □ What constitutes lawful industrial action? □ Trade union negotiations □ Further information and advice

Why is consultation important?

Small firms are in a position to enjoy excellent employee relations. Staff are likely to display a strong sense of belonging to the firm, they are likely to be on first name terms with each other, and problems can be dealt with quickly on a face to face basis.

Even so, particularly for the growing firm, it is important that a two-way communication channel exists. To prevent the spreading of misinformation and rumour, staff should be systematically consulted and regularly informed of:

- changes in conditions of employment, pay, hours of work, holidays, etc.
- changes in who does what job
- changes in the way jobs are carried out
- the firm's progress.

A basic procedure should also exist through which employees raise any problems they may have, for example, on working conditions or pay. This will enable management to deal with problems on an open basis preventing the bottling up of tension and its possible consequences, high absenteeism and labour turnover. See section on staff grievances in Chap. 5.

What communication methods should be used?

Verbal communication

Face-to-face communication is the simplest method, and this is particularly suitable for the smaller firm. Meetings may take place on an individual basis, more or less informally (see performance appraisal, Chap. 3), or on a group basis for management to communicate information and gain a response to it. In the very small firm, regular meetings of the whole company will be possible, but for the larger organization, staff will need to be broken down into sub-units to enable effective discussion to take place.

On certain issues, you may not wish to get involved in discussion, for example, if giving notice of impending redundancy. In this case, an announcement to the whole firm could be the best method.

Written communication

If management is seeking to provide information for reference purposes, and accuracy is important in such cases, then a written communication method should be used. There are also instances when employees have a legal entitlement to receiving information in written form. See Chap. 9.

A number of possibilities exist.

Employee handbooks

Brief information to all staff on what the firm does, its facilities, basic employment conditions and rules.

Reports to staff

Information on the activities and performance of the firm, containing profit figures, etc.

Reference papers

For detailed information which has a long period of applicability, for example, on the system of payment, factory or office rules, disciplinary procedure, methods of safe working, arrangements for maternity leave.

Memoranda and circulars

For specific items, which are of contemporary relevance. Can be directed towards concerned individuals only.

Noticeboards

Can be used to convey various items of information. They should not be cluttered and notices should be removed immediately after they cease to be relevant so that new ones are not ignored.

What is a trade union?

A trade union is an organization which exists to represent the interests of employees and the regulation of relations between the employees and the employer. Trade unions range in size, from the huge concerns representing over a million workers to the smaller unions representing a hundred or so workers.

A union represents a particular type of worker and since any business, regardless of size, includes many different types of workers, it is usual for the workers in one organization to be represented by a number of different unions. Senior managers tend not to belong to unions due to conflict of interest.

The employees' contact with the union in the workplace is the shop steward. The shop steward is elected by union members in the firm to be their representative and spokesperson. He or she will represent union members in all dealings with management. The union members are attached to a local branch, which elects representatives to a regional committee. The policy of the union is implemented by another elected committee, the national committee. The union employs permanent staff at regional and headquarters level.

Trade unions and the small business

One of the main reasons why employees join trade unions is because they want to try to improve their working conditions and try to affect their working environment. In large organizations trade unions provide a means by which the voice of the workers can be heard. With highly structured management systems and often inadequate communication with workers, employees feel the need to organize themselves on a more formal basis.

With the more friendly working environment of the small business and the close working relations between 'management' (i.e., you) and 'the workforce', the problems of isolation and poor communication are much rarer. Employees have the opportunity to talk to the owner of the small business, to offer advice and to be kept informed of developments and the progress of the business.

It is, therefore, less likely that your employees will want to join a union. If you hear mention of the possibility, this is the time to ask yourself whether you are perhaps neglecting some aspects of your personnel management. Ask employees how they are getting on and whether they have any problems they wish to discuss. The great advantage you have over larger organizations is that you are in the position to react quickly, if employees have what you feel are justifiable grievances. The value of this flexibility should not be underestimated.

The introduction of trade union organization will have a profound effect on the way you run your business:

- Many of the decisions you make will be subject to challenge and unions will have to be consulted before decisions are implemented.
- The presence of the union will impinge on your right to manage.
- You will no longer be able to communicate directly with employees regarding terms and conditions of employment which are subject to negotiation with the union.
- If pay scales are introduced, you will be restricted in your ability to grant individuals pay increases because you feel they deserve them.
- Union negotiations are often time consuming and do require expertise. You will therefore have to assign time to this, when the time would otherwise have been spent running the business.

The advantages which union organization brings to larger companies, e.g., only one set of negotiators to deal with, improved employee communication, etc., will not apply to the owner of the small business. The effect on the running of the small business, on the other hand, could have a serious impact on the business' essential ability to adapt quickly to changing circumstances.

It must be said, however, that not all owners of small businesses operate in a way which enables employees to work in a friendly, positive environment. In these cases, the unions play an important role in representing employees' interests.

Handling trade unions

You cannot be forced by law to recognize a trade union. If you are approached by a large percentage of your employees regarding union recognition, however, you would be very foolish to refuse outright and to consider the matter closed. The resulting damage to staff morale and possible withdrawal of co-operation on which your business depends could have serious effects.

If a union is to be recognized, you should adopt a positive approach to ensure that the possible adverse effects of collective bargaining are minimized. Consider the following:

- Recognizing only one union does have the advantage of there being only one set of negotiations. If all the union members in the company belong to one union you are also less likely to have demarcation problems. However, if there is only one union representing your employees, that union is in a very strong position. Having more than one union is more time consuming, but does reduce the power of the individual unions.
- You do not have to negotiate all aspects of the workers' terms and conditions with the trade union. You are entitled to restrict the number of negotiable issues, e.g. exclusion of pay.
- You should try to keep union negotiations internal as far as possible and use external representatives only as a last resort.
- In small businesses it is sometimes possible to enter into a no-strike agreement with a union. It is obviously not in the employees' interests for the business to fail and in many small businesses a strike would cause this to happen before too long. If this is not possible, try to negotiate an agreement that outside arbitrators, such as ACAS, will be called in, before strike action is taken.

The closed shop

A closed shop is an agreement made between you and union representatives to the effect that, with a few exceptions, all employees will be required to join the recognized union(s).

New closed shop agreements should have the overwhelming support (more than 80%) of those to be covered, expressed in a secret ballot. Individuals who do not wish to join any trade union on grounds of conscience or other deeply held personal convictions cannot be compelled to do so and cannot be dismissed as a result. Individuals who were not union members at the time the closed shop agreement was made cannot be compelled to become members. Please refer to current legislation for more details on the legality of closed shops.

Guidelines for employee representation

ACAS (The Arbitration, Conciliation & Advisory Service) have published the following guidelines for employee representation in small businesses.

1. A simple written negotiating procedure should be established probably containing no more than three stages for example:

   (*a*) Shop steward may raise issue with first line manager.
   (*b*) If no agreement, managing director will meet shop steward and union officer.
   (*c*) If no agreement, the parties may request conciliation or arbitration.

2. Bargaining arrangements should be made clear:

   (*a*) How and when can meetings be arranged?
   (*b*) Who will attend meeting and who will do the negotiating?
   (*c*) What facilities will be available to union representatives – telephone, notice board, stationery etc?
   (*d*) How much time will be made available to union representatives and members for trade union duties, meetings and other trade union activities?
   (*e*) How should agreements and disagreements be made known to employees?

3. Neither party should be in any doubt about what matters are to be the subject of joint agreement. They may typically include pay and payment systems, hours of work, holiday sick pay provisions, premium payments (e.g. bonus, overtime, shift), security of employment.

4. On occasions when agreements cannot be reached during negotiations, either or both parties may want to use the independent conciliation service of ACAS. If agreement still cannot be reached through negotiation, then at the joint request of the parties, ACAS may appoint an independent arbitrator, provided both sides agree to be bound by his decision.

What are the rights of recognised trade unions?

Union rights is a complex and often confusing area. What follows is a very brief guide for those involved in union negotiations, but should you need a fuller treatment, please refer to *Croner's Reference Book for Employers* (see Chap. 9).

- To appoint safety representatives (see Health and Safety Commission publication *Safety Representatives and Safety Committees*).
- To receive information for collective bargaining purposes (see ACAS Code of Practice 2: *Disclosure of information to trade unions for collective bargaining purposes*). Typical information would be on

current levels of pay, financial information, company performance information, manning figures.

- To be consulted over redundancy and transference of the business (see Department of Employment booklet no. 2 *Procedures for Handling Redundancies* and booklet no. 10 *Employee Rights on Transfer of Undertaking*).
- To obtain public funds for ballots relating to the election of key officials and industrial action.
- Officials are allowed time off work with pay (ACAS Code of Practice 3: *Time off for trade union duties and activities*), and access to reasonable facilities, e.g. stationery, photocopying.
- Agreements made with trade unions are not legally binding, unless there has been a special agreement to this effect. Agreements on terms and conditions of employment can however become part of the individual's Contract of Employment which is legally binding. Obviously there are other reasons why employers will be reluctant to fail to honour agreements with unions.

What are the rights of trade union members?

- Not to have action taken against them to prevent trade union membership.
- To receive reasonable time off work (unpaid, unless a union official, or there is an agreement to the contrary) to take part in trade union activities.
- Not to be unreasonably excluded from, or expelled by, a trade union.
- Not to be dismissed on grounds of trade union activities.

What constitutes lawful industrial action?

- The action can only be taken against a company which is *directly* involved in the dispute. *Secondary* activity is not lawful.
- The action must be directly connected with terms and conditions of employment, discipline or dismissal, work allocation, or the operation of negotiating and consultative machinery.
- The action must be based on a secret ballot of trade union members which results in a majority in favour of it.
- The small firm is not under an obligation to provide facilities or premises for the organization and administration of industrial action by trade unions.

Trade union negotiations

Having recognized a trade union, you will then become involved in negotiations to draw up a statement of terms and conditions for employees with the union(s) representing the employees and the management representing the business. If possible, it is preferable for the owner of the business or the managing director not to be directly involved in negotiations. He or she can be the fall-back position, to which the others can come if they reach deadlock.

The statement of terms and conditions can be either quite short and basic and negotiable on an annual basis or quite a long and complex document, which once drawn up will not then be negotiable. There are certain standard agreements available. Avoid these at all costs. It is essential that the agreement is appropriate to your business, tailor-made to fit the requirements of your company.

There are three stages to a negotiating process: preparation, the meetings, the agreement.

Preparation

It is essential that you prepare properly for these meetings. If you are not adequately prepared, postpone the meeting.

- Agree an agenda. You will have been approached by the union representatives and you will have discussed what is to be on the agenda of the meeting.
- Check facts and figures and have back-up documentation to hand. For example, in pay negotiations, you should check local and comparabale rates of pay, the retail price index (the rate of inflation which will affect *actual* wage increases), company profitability, relevant statutory pensions. Always be fully briefed regarding employees' current terms and conditions.
- Select the information to be disclosed to trade union negotiators. Compile in simple form.
- Prepare your own case – arguments and reasons for them. Attach priorities to issues. Which would you least like to concede?
- If possible, liaise informally with union negotiators to gain a picture of their 'demand'.
- Communicate *directly* with staff through regular meetings and other communication methods on background issues pertaining to the negotiations.

- Give attention to seating arrangements, refreshments, etc. Decide on the venue for the negotiations.
- If there is to be a management negotiating team, ensure that there is internal agreement. Establish roles, for example lead spokesman, financial expert.

The negotiations

This is a very protracted series of meetings, probably stretching over a considerable period of time. To negotiate a totally new house agreement could take up to a year. It is essential that minutes are taken at each meeting, that these are checked and reviewed at the beginning of the following meeting. Each meeting will probably have three stages:

Stage 1

Ascertain the union's demand. Possible recess to review position.

Stage 2

Put forward management's offer with reasons. Do not begin with your final offer. For example, if you know that the most you can afford is a 5% pay increase, offer 3% at first. The offer should be realistic, however. One person should be charged with presenting management's case. Possible recess to review position.

Stage 3

Explore possibilities for compromise. Seek to identify those areas in which the union is willing to make a concession and link management concessions to these. Make tentative suggestions without commitment.

Always substantiate arguments with facts and figures, where appropriate. Experts may speak on certain key areas, e.g., financial or employment aspects. Throughout this stage, there may be frequent recesses.

Agreement

Now move towards making *definite* commitments and gaining commitments in return.

Record agreements in writing and obtain the confirmation of union negotiators as to the content of this statement. Arrange for the communication of the statement to all employees.

Further information and advice

There are several organizations to whom you can turn if you need to help with negotiations or advice on any aspect of personnel management.

The Arbitration, Conciliation and Advisory Service (ACAS)

ACAS is an independent body which offers free advice on matters concerned with employee relations and assistance to parties in industrial disputes.

This is a highly respected organization by unions and employers alike. They publish codes of practice and guidelines for employers.

The Industrial Society

This is another source of useful advice and information on all aspects of personnel work. The subscriptions vary according to the size of business which is a major advantage to small companies. The society runs training courses and advice services.

The Institute of Personnel Managers (IPM)

If you are a member of the IPM, you have access to a wide range of advice and information services, training courses, etc.

Action checklist

- Make sure staff are informed of all important matters affecting them, either by using a variety of written media, or verbal methods.
- Set up a basic procedure to ensure staff problems are picked up and dealt with quickly.
- Consider seriously requests for union recognition.
- When dealing with union negotiators follow three main stages:
  (*a*) prepare thoroughly
  (*b*) discuss without commitment
  (*c*) if necessary, compromise to reach a definite settlement.

7 Parting with staff

Terminating the contract □ Redundancy □ Dismissing staff □ When can employee claim unfair dismissal □ Other forms of dismissal

This may very well be the first chapter you have turned to, as more problems arise for managers when parting with staff than in any other area of dealing with people. However well you manage your staff, any number of situations can make termination of the contract the only option.

The law relating to the termination of employment is covered by common law and aspects of statute law. In this chapter we shall be looking at both with particular reference to:

- Rights of notice.
- Redundancy.
- Dismissal.

The statutory provisions are now contained in the Employment Protection (Consolidation) Act 1978 and the Employment Act 1980, having been brought together from various pieces of earlier legislation.

Terminating the contract

The contract of employment may be terminated by either party, that is either by you, as the employer, or by the employee. The circumstances surrounding the termination of employment may vary considerably, e.g. the employee may resign or retire (the law makes no distinctions here), or you may decide to make the employee redundant or in fact dismiss him or her.

Notice required from employees

An employee who has been continuously employed for four weeks or more is required by law to give his or her employer at least one week's notice in writing to terminate the contract of employment. However, this does not increase with service.

If an employee accepts a contract in which the notice periods that have to be given are longer he or she is bound by that contract although the employer may have problems enforcing this. Any redress would be to the local county courts. This is not normally a cost effective method.

If an employee resigns and then changes his or her mind, this can only be done if the employer agrees that the contract of employment may remain in existence. Equally if the employer gives notice to an employee and wishes later to withdraw it, this can only be done if the employee agrees that the contract of employment is to remain in existence.

Notice required from employers

The length of notice which employers must give employees depends on how long the employee has been working for the company.

Service	*Notice required*
After one month's service	One week
After two years' service	Two weeks
After three years' service	Three weeks
and so on, to a maximum of	
After twelve years' service	Twelve weeks

These are minimum periods of notice. If the contract of employment specifies a longer period, then that period applies.

Redundancy

Under the Employment Protection (Consolidation) Act 1978, redundancy is presumed to occur where the services of employees are dispensed with because the employer ceases, or intends to cease, carrying on business, or to carry on business at the place where the employee was employed, or does not require so many employees to do a certain kind of work. Redundancies may, therefore, arise when jobs cease to exist due to a decline in the activity of the business, or through some form of internal reorganization. The loss of staff it entails can be potentially very damaging, and individuals made redundant are likely to find the experience very stressful. However, if handled sensibly and systematically, the adverse effects of redundancy can be minimized. It should be remembered that the loss of a few jobs can and often does save other jobs elsewhere in the firm.

If the redundancy situation is anticipated, you can take action to run down staffing levels, and thus avoid having to compel employees to leave.

Possibility	*Effect*
Halt recruitment	Stops flow of 'new blood' into firm
Early retirement	Valuable experience may be lost
Job sharing	Those not affected by redundancy may resist curtailment of their job
Reducing or eliminating overtime	Reduces management flexibility to meet manning levels
Termination of employment of temporary staff	Reduces management flexibility to meet manning levels
Retaining or transfer of staff	Could create a 'gap' elsewhere unless individual covers two jobs

Alternatively, you can seek volunteers for redundancy. This will be an expensive option as an adequate cash incentive needs to be offered to leavers. Also, it is important that you consider future manning requirements when deciding whether or not to encourage a volunteer to leave. Clearly you need to retain key skills and a balance of youth and experience.

How should redundancies be implemented?

(See also Chap. 9.) Sometimes, it will be impossible to avoid the implementation of redundancies, in which case you should pay attention to the following points:

- Communicate with affected employees over the redundancies as soon as possible. Give them as much notice as possible. Ensure that knowledge of the redundancy situation does not become public before the employees themselves are informed. Also notify the Department of Employment and any recognized trade unions within specified time limits.
- Provide affected employees with reasonable time during working hours to look for new employment or make arrangements for training. This is their legal entitlement.
- Ensure a fair and agreed method is used for selecting staff for redundancy. This is your legal duty. Criteria for selection should include length of service, standards of performance, suitability for retraining.
- Prior to making redundancies you should, therefore, stop recruitment, ban overtime, introduce short-working and insist that all employees over normal retirement age retire. Try also, to find volunteers for

redundancy. As far as possible, try to cut down the workforce through natural wastage rather than by compulsion.

- Consult with remaining staff to ensure that their morale is not adversely affected by the redundancies.
- Inform the local Job Centre and local employers of skills possessed by redundant staff.
- Post suitable job vacancies on noticeboards.
- Where feasible, provide practical assistance to redundant employees such as typing and photocopying facilities.
- On termination of employment for staff with two or more years' service, provide them with a lump sum payment relating to age, length of service and pay, and with a written statement showing how this was calculated. (Standard procedures for this are outlined by the Institute of Personnel Managers in their *Redundancy Code*.)

Dismissing staff

You have turned to this page because you feel you have come to the end of the road with an employee. When dismissing an employee, you should control any emotional or personal feelings that you have towards the individual. In most cases, when an employee is dismissed, there are very sound reasons for the decision being taken. It is usually straightforward, although never pleasant.

Later in this chapter, we shall discuss unfair dismissal, the role of industrial tribunals and related matters. However, if you follow the correct procedures when dismissing an employee, then you should never find yourself in the unfortunate position of being involved in these matters.

Under current legislation, there are several circumstances in which it may be fair to dismiss an employee. These are:

- poor performance or inability to perform job for which the employee has been recruited
- unsatisfactory conduct
- redundancy
- the continuation of employment would contravene the law
- other substantial reasons.

When handling disciplinary matters and possible dismissals, the most important first step is to gather together the facts of the matter. If the problem has been reported to you by another employee, it is particularly important for you to look into the problem yourself, and the background to the problem. The facts you should consider are:

- What has the employee done wrong?
- How long has the employee been doing the job?
- Does the employee understand what is expected?
- Has someone talked to the employee about performance?
- Has the employee been given the opportunity to improve?
- Does the employee require training?
- What are the advantages of employing this person?
- What are the disadvantages of employing this person?
- Is the employee best suited to another role within the company?
- Do you have another role to offer the employee?
- Are you sure you are acting within the law?
- What will be the effects on the morale of other employees, if the employee is dismissed/is retained?

New recruits

If the employee has only recently been recruited into the firm it may be that there has been a *two-way* error at the recruitment stage. Normally an employee will settle into a role within two to three months of joining the firm. However, his or her perception at the interview stage of what needs to be done to meet the requirements of the position and the firm's perception of the individual's ability at the interview may have been wrong – hence, two-way. See Chap. 2 for further discussion of probationary periods.

Experienced employees

If the employee has been with you for some time and is now not performing, you should consider the following:

- Has the job changed in any way, e.g. the demands become greater over the last few years?
- Is there some personal reason why the employee is not performing?
- Has the employee recently been promoted? Is there any further training needed for this position?

If you have answered no to each of the above, then the problem is not a short term one and will need to be dealt with.

At all times, when dealing with a long serving employee, you should consider the effects terminating the employment contract will have on the morale of other employees. Most of the employee's colleagues, if you are acting reasonably and fairly as an employer, will not feel their own job security is threatened by your actions. However, if you are not acting fairly or fall outside the law, you will create further management problems for yourself within the firm. Morale problems can also arise when a person is maintained in a position and is not performing satisfactorily. Resentment from colleagues will set in as they will feel that the employee has been treated with favouritism, is 'getting away with it'.

A long serving employee is more difficult to deal with as personal feelings become more involved with the employee, and particularly in small businesses the employee normally feels very loyal and committed to the firm. However, at the end of the day you must consider that you are running a business where non-performance can greatly affect the future of the firm.

Does the employee understand what is expected of him or her?

You should at all times question whether the employee understands what is expected of him or her. In most cases the employee will probably understand what is expected but will not be capable of doing it. You should ensure, however, that this is understood. It is often sensible at the early stages of disciplinary procedure to reissue a list of the duties (job description) that the employee is expected to perform and any measures or standards associated with it, e.g., to pack tape measures in boxes. A minimum standard of 50 boxes a day to be completed.

Has someone talked to the employee about performance?

It is often very surprising how many people actually believe that they have talked to an individual about performance and the individual has no idea that he or she has been talked to. Most people avoid confrontation when there is something unpleasant to be said. Talking to an individual about his or her performance does not necessarily have to be unpleasant. In fact avoiding talking to an individual can have much more damaging effects than being straightforward and honest. As explained earlier, it is your responsibility as an employer to ensure that the employee knows exactly what you expect. There are no half measures in talking to an individual about performance.

The disciplinary procedure

Once you have collected together all the facts and decided that disciplinary action is warranted, you should then adopt a disciplinary procedure that is objective and will treat the employee in a fair and reasonable manner. You may find that having been disciplined, the employee takes great pains to improve performance and the problem need go no further.

The disciplinary procedure has four stages.

Formal oral warning

This will generally follow one or more informal warnings and discussions. A note will be kept on the personnel file that an oral warning has been given, including the date and the subject concerned.

First written warning

This stage is reached after there has been no significant improvement following an oral warning, or where the matter is serious enough to justify omitting the oral warning.

Final written warning

This follows a first (or occasionally a second/follow up) written warning when no improvement has been noted, or when the situation is judged to be extremely serious and inappropriate for early stages of warning. This stage may be omitted if the offence is considered serious enough.

Dismissal

This follows a continuing serious situation that does not improve. In exceptional circumstances summary or instant dismissal may follow an occurrence of gross misconduct and in this case the employee has no entitlement to pay in lieu of notice or to accrued holiday pay.

At all stages of the disciplinary procedures, the employee should have the right to appeal against any warnings or action being taken. It is therefore sensible to have a written appeal procedure for your company (see Chap. 5).

The disciplinary procedure is discussed in greater detail in Chap. 5.

Dismissing an employee

If, after the final written warning, the employee's performance still does not improve and he or she has no satisfactory explanation, then you must terminate his or her contract. If you allow the employee to continue without taking action, his or her performance will never improve and this may have a damaging effect on other employees. Moreover, it may make a subsequent dismissal more likely to be judged as unfair.

Firing an employee is never easy, and can be a very emotional experience. However, after you have reached this stage, the employee will know what the outcome is going to be and will therefore probably be resigned to the fact anyway. If you have reached the decision to terminate the employee's contract, you should not at this stage accept a resignation from the employee as this later could be construed as constructive dismissal (see later in this chapter).

It is obviously better if, before you reach this stage, you can mutually agree that the employee should leave. However, in some cases this will not be possible. At this final interview you should explain the reasons for your decision to terminate the contract and give the employee notice. In most cases it will be sensible to allow the employee to leave straight away with payment in lieu of notice and accrued holiday pay. However, in some circumstances the employee can work notice. You should consider the damaging effects of having an employee on the premises who knows that he or she is leaving.

After the employee has left, you should calculate any pay as necessary (see Chap. 4), forward any payments due to the employee with a covering letter explaining the reasons for dismissal. You do not legally have to explain your reasons for dismissal in a letter unless requested to do so by the employee. However, it would seem sensible to do this as clearly and accurately as possible. You should also explain in this letter the position regarding references for the employee. If the employee has worked for the company for more than two years, you should draw attention to the fact that if he or she feels unfairly treated, redress can be sought at an industrial tribunal. See specimen letter in Fig. 7.1.

Gross misconduct and summary dismissal

In cases of serious misconduct an employee may be subject to summary dismissal, which means immediate termination of employment without notice and without entitlement to accrued holiday pay. This should not be confused with payment of notice and holiday pay which may occur at the company's discretion in certain cases of dismissal resulting from the normal disciplinary procedures.

Summary dismissal can result from a single occurrence of serious misconduct and does not require completion of the warning procedure.

Summary dismissal should not be used as a means of avoiding disciplinary procedures. Care must be taken to ensure that you are seen to be fair and that the situation warrants termination of contract. Industrial tribunals will take a dim view of employers who do not consider the consequences of summary dismissal. (See Chap. 8.)

Dear ....,

With reference to our recent meeting I am writing to confirm the firm's decision to terminate your contract with effect from ....

As explained to you at this meeting the reasons for your dismissal are as follows:

(Fill in the reasons for dismissal)

I have enclosed your final payslip and your P45.

As explained at our meeting the firm will be prepared to give you a fair and honest reference.

If you feel that the firm's action has been unfair then your redress will be through an industrial tribunal. Obviously you should take individual counsel as to your rights. However I would stress that any action to an industrial tribunal should be taken within a three-month period of leaving the firm or you will lose your right to appeal.

Please feel free to contact me directly, should you have any queries relating to this or your final pay settlement.

Yours sincerely,

R Jones
Director

Fig. 7.1 A specimen letter of termination of contract

Suspension

There are two types of suspension:

(*a*) Investigative suspension. You can reserve the right to suspend an employee on basic pay in case of a suspected serious misconduct, pending further investigation or a decision being made at a higher level of management. It will normally be followed either by disciplinary action or withdrawal of allegations relating to the incident.
(*b*) Disciplinary suspension. This may be used as part of the disciplinary procedure as an extra stage to impress on an employee the seriousness of the situation. It will not be used automatically, but anywhere it is judged to be appropriate. Disciplinary suspension can be without pay if this is agreed in the contract of employment, and will normally be between one and three days. Disciplinary suspension should only be authorized by senior management.

Examples of disciplinary regulations and reasons for dismissal

You may find the list below of help. The rules and reasons listed here are not exhaustive, but show examples of the main occurrences which will give rise to the disciplinary measures indicated. These rules should apply to all employees, but each case should be considered carefully on its own merits and the prevailing circumstances.

Minor disciplinary situations

The following will normally be treated informally at first, but repeated occurrences will justify the formal warning procedure:

- unexcused lateness
- excessive break times
- careless behaviour
- failure to wear suitable clothes or present a suitable appearance
- unexcused absence or failure to notify the company correctly
- failure to observe instructions or follow agreed procedures or policies.

Serious disciplinary situations

The following are serious offences which normally will be dealt with by a formal warning procedure:

- unexcused absence without notification
- excessive absence (not certified sickness) with or without notification
- committing a series of unsatisfactory actions within a short period of time
- failure to observe health and safety rules
- performing work other than for the company during paid time
- preventing another employee from carrying out his or her duties effectively
- working in unauthorized areas
- damage to company property
- failure to report an accident or dangerous occurrence at work.

Major disciplinary situations

For these situations the severity of disciplinary action will depend on the circumstances. Disciplinary suspension or a final warning may be an immediate first stage or the warning procedure may be otherwise condensed:

- offences under summary dismissal where there are substantial mitigating circumstances
- deliberate refusal to carry out a legitimate job instruction
- disorderly conduct on the premises
- gross negligence
- use of abusive or offensive language or behaviour
- breach of confidence/company security or confidentiality.

Summary dismissal

The following are examples of circumstances which could be considered as gross misconduct and serious enough to justify summary dismissal treatment. If you decide to use the examples for your own firm these should be adjusted and amended and a copy contained within your company reference document. Items listed under 2 below may also be considered under this heading, if the circumstances are particularly grey.

- unauthorized possession or use of company property or money belonging to the company, to other employees or to members of the public. The value of the money or the property will have no effect on the disciplinary action taken but may influence any decisions about taking legal proceedings
- falsification, including deliberate omissions, of company records or procedures where this results in material gain to the employee (e.g., bonus figures, weekly/monthly figures, substances and expense claims)
- serious incapability through excessive use of alcohol or drugs and unauthorized possession of drugs whilst on company premises or in working time.
- conviction or arrest on a serious criminal charge which affects the employee's ability/acceptability to remain in employment or where the offence has occurred on company premises
- use of violence towards other persons or property, or destruction or abuse of machinery or equipment
- the use of obscene language or behaviour or gross insubordination, particularly in the presence of others
- deliberate contravention of health and safety regulations, especially where this involves smoking in unauthorized places where this is a serious fire hazard
- unauthorized disclosure of highly confidential matters

- gross negligence or extremely irresponsible behaviour
- failure to follow provisions as laid down in any acts applicable to the type of work you perform, e.g., Estate Agents Act: confidentiality in case of solicitors, etc.
- unauthorized possession of an offensive weapon.

Written statement of reasons

After an employee has been employed for 26 weeks and is then dismissed, if requested by the employee to do so, the employer must provide a written statement within 14 days of the reasons for the employee's dismissal. If you fail to do this or the statement is false, then the employee may be eligible to take the matter to an industrial tribunal. If the tribunal finds the complaint justified it will award the employee two week's pay. When writing a statement you should always ensure that the reasons are honest and unambiguous. In these instances, it is better not to spare the feelings of an employee as later the employee may use this in an industrial tribunal. The right to a proper statement of reasons is independent of the right not to be unfairly dismissed.

When can an employee claim unfair dismissal?

An employee who believes that he or she has been unfairly dismissed has the right to lodge a complaint with an industrial tribunal.

Those eligible are:

- an employee who has been continually employed by an employer for at least two years on a full-time basis
- an employee who works sixteen or more hours a week or has worked for the employer continuously for five years and works between eight and sixteen hours a week
- an employee who is under 65 (60 for women) or below the normal retirement age for this type of employment. Following a recent House of Lords appeal hearing, it is reasonable to conclude that the age which will apply in future to both men and women will be 65 (an exception will be made for uniformed fire and police services)
- an employee who makes a claim within three months of dismissal. Only very exceptionally will a late application be considered.

Dismissal of an employee is automatically deemed to be unfair when:

- an employee is dismissed because she is pregnant or for a reason connected with her pregnancy
- an employee is dismissed for a conviction which he or she has spent under the Rehabilitation of Offenders Act
- an employee is dismissed for various inadmissible reasons, the term used to describe situations where the employer dismisses an employee for belonging to a trade union or participating in its activities.

The most important feature of these inadmissible reasons is the applicant does not have to complete a qualifying period of continuous service or could even lodge a complaint after normal retirement age for his work.

The rights of these people have been laid down by various Acts of Parliament. For further detail, see Trade Union Relations Act 1974, the Employment Protection Act 1975, re-enacted in the Employment Protection (Consolidation) Act 1978, and the Employment Acts 1980 and 1982.

Those excluded

The following workers are excluded from the right to lodge a complaint with an industrial tribunal:

- registered dockworkers
- a master or a member of the crew of a fishing vessel where employees are not renumerated otherwise than by a share in the profits or gross earnings of the vessel
- employees who under contract normally work outside Great Britain
- employees working under fixed terms of contract of one year or more, who have agreed in writing to exclude any claim for unfair dismissal, where dismissal consists of the expiry of the fixed term without it being renewed.

What are industrial tribunals?

Industrial tribunals have jurisdiction to decide most disputes over individual employee rights: unfair dismissal, redundancy, sex discrimination, maternity payments, etc. There is a legally qualified chairperson and two other members chosen for their experience as employers or trade unionists. Tribunals sit locally; proceedings are relatively informal but you have to produce your own witnesses and documents to prove your case. The tribunal does not arbitrate but applies the law.

Anybody can represent parties before industrial tribunals. Employees are often represented by trade union officials, but you can have legal representation if you wish. Legal aid is not available. Costs are almost never recoverable and employees have little disincentive to pursue weak cases. Although it is up to an employee to bring his or her case to tribunal, it is often up to employer to *disprove* a claim. If you find yourself involved in this type of situation, it is advisable to contact ACAS.

Employment appeal tribunals

These are special courts. They hear appeals *on questions of law* from industrial tribunals. The court consists of a high court judge and two lay members with industrial experience. Since it only deals with legal questions, legal advice is essential, but representation by a lawyer is not obligatory.

What does the industrial tribunal consider?

Tribunal members are concerned with precedents and fairness for employment as a whole, not within one industrial concentration. In looking at whether a dismissal is fair, the industrial tribunal must first decide that an employee has been dismissed. The onus is on the employee to prove that he or she has been dismissed. Dismissal and dismissed are defined as follows:

- if the contract under which an employee is employed by an employer is terminated by the employer, whether or not it is terminated by notice, or
- if, where an employee is employed under contract for a fixed term, the term expires without being renewed under the same contract, or
- the employee is entitled to terminate the contract (through resignation) with or without notice because of circumstances caused by the employer's conduct, i.e. when the employer behaves in a manner that demonstrates refusal to be bound by the contract of employment. This is termed 'constructive dismissal' and means that the employer has behaved in such a way as to force the employee to resign.

The industrial tribunal will look at:

The substantive aspects

For example, in the case of poor time-keeping the employer would have to show that his or her reasons for dismissal were for that particular act of misconduct (this may be difficult). An employer cannot latch on to a trivial reason and rely upon that. An employer has to be seen to be fair to the employee.

Procedural safeguards

The second aspect that an industrial tribunal will look at is the procedural safeguards which have been developed by courts and tribunals that show the employer has acted reasonably. The most important procedural aspect used is that of the ACAS Code of Practice 1: *Disciplinary practice and procedures in employment*, which states that an individual has a right to a warning (normally a first verbal warning and then a written warning), that an individual has a right to state his or her case before being dismissed, that an individual has the ability to explain his or her actions, that the employee should have the right to appeal against the decision within the organization.

It does not mean, however, that because you do not follow the procedural safeguards that a dismissal will automatically be seen as unfair. However, the tribunal does still put a lot of emphasis on the employers acting reasonably.

The tribunal is therefore seen to test the fairness of the employer's decisions and actions. In the past, when unfair dismissal has been proved, the compensation given to employees has not by and large been high. This does not mean, however, that an employer should ignore the law. It should be remembered that the repercussions of an unfair dismissal case for an employer will be felt within the firm by the employees that remain and also outside the firm by the way that the firm is viewed by its business contacts and the public at large.

What then are the powers of the industrial tribunal?

Once the industrial tribunal has found a dismissal to be unfair, it can consider various remedies. These basically fall into three categories: reinstatement, re-engagement or compensation.

Reinstatement or re-engagement

With reinstatement, the employee is treated as if he or she has never been dismissed, in all respects. This will include pay, holiday, pension contributions, etc. It may well be, however, that it is not practical to reinstate the employee in the job that he or she was doing before the industrial tribunal.

The tribunal therefore can consider re-engagement of the employee, i.e. the provision of another position within the business for the employee. The job must be suitable employment and unless the employee has partly contributed to the dismissal, re-engagement must be on the terms which are as far as possible as favourable as those he or she left. Obviously, the tribunal will take into consideration factors such as whether the employee wants to be reinstated, whether it is practical for the employee to be reinstated, or whether the employee has caused or contributed to the reason for dismissal. If after an industrial tribunal has ordered an employer to re-engage or reinstate an employee and he refuses, the tribunal will consider compensationary awards.

Compensation

This normally falls into two areas: basic compensation and compensationary award. *Basic compensation* is normally equivalent to the statutory redundancy compensation an employee would have received if he or she had been made redundant. The loss of job security will also be taken into account. Again, the industrial tribunal will consider whether an employee has contributed to the dismissal. The *compensationary award* is designed to compensate the employee for financial loss that he or she has incurred due to unfair dismissal. The tribunal will look at one of three factors when assessing this award:

- whether or not an employee is likely to find a new job
- whether or not there was any loss at all (i.e. the employment may have ceased anyway)
- limited future loss whereby an employee may have been dismissed shortly anyway.

Other forms of dismissal

Constructive dismissal

If, as an employer you behave in such a way that an employee is forced to resign, this is known as constructive dismissal. If constructive dismissal can be proved, you as an employer are liable. The type of behaviour that might justify such action is when there are changes in the basic terms of conditions originally offered to the employee, e.g., change in status, pay, benefits, working arrangements or place of work. The conduct of both parties is looked at when assessing whether or not an employer's conduct was such that an employee was entitled to say that he or she was forced to go.

Through the Employment Protection (Consolidation) Act 1978, the employer's position was somewhat strengthened by the decision that for an employee to prove constructive dismissal he or she has to prove substantial breach of contract by the employer. An example of a case that was held was an instance where an employee employed by a construction company was moved to a different location. He left the job and claimed to be constructively dismissed because his work place had changed. His claim was upheld on the grounds that it was not contained within his contract of employment that he should be mobile.

These cases are also referred to industrial tribunals.

Constructive resignation

The employee can behave in such a way that the employer can reasonably assume that he or she has resigned although no formal resignation has been received. Again, for constructive resignation to be established there must be a clear breach of the terms of contract and for it to be shown that the employee does not wish to continue to be bound by that contract. An example of this would be unauthorized absence where an employee repeatedly fails to attend work or give reasons for not attending work. If, after repeated attempts, the employee cannot be contacted, the employer can write to the employee explaining that if he or she does not hear from the employee by a certain date it will be assumed that the employee has resigned from the company. See specimen letter in Fig. 7.2. These cases are referred to industrial tribunals.

Wrongful dismissal

If the employer fails to give the notice required under the contract of employment (or wages in lieu of notice), then the employee could bring an action of wrongful dismissal (not unfair dismissal) in ordinary court. Normally, the notice which the employer would be required to give would be the minimum period of notice stipulated in the contract of employment. Compensation available would normally amount to the amount the employee would have received if he had not been wrongfully dismissed. To be able to claim for wrongful dismissal the employee must have over four weeks' service, unless the contract of employment provides otherwise.

It would be wise to send this letter by registered mail to ensure the employee has received it.

Dear ....,

We have tried to contact you on several occasions without success over the last two weeks to establish the reasons for your not attending work.

We are obviously concerned as to your welfare. However, as you have made no attempt to contact us we can only assume that you have decided not to continue employment with us.

If we do not hear from you therefore by Monday 3 August we will assume that you wish to terminate your contract with effect from Friday 17 July 1987, being the last day you worked with us.

I am sorry to have reached this decision. However, I am sure you appreciate that the situation cannot continue. If you have decided to resign, I would still very much like to be able to contact you so that we can talk through the reasons for your decision.

I look forward to hearing from you.

Yours sincerely,

R Jones
Director

Fig. 7.2 A specimen letter to an employee who has failed to attend work

8 Keeping records

Personnel files □ Reference book

There are various records that you are legally obliged to keep on such things as pay, statutory sick pay and maternity pay. These have been dealt with in Chap. 4. However, there are also other areas of records that should be kept on individual employees.

Personnel files

You should set up a personnel file for each employee which contains personal information on the employee. These should at all times be kept under lock and key. You should not divulge information outside the firm on the employees without their prior consent. There are two methods which you could use to maintain these records: manual and computerized. If you hold this information on computer you should ensure that you are complying with the Data Protection Act (see Chap. 9).

Information normally held on employees

Details should include: name, age, address, date of birth, children, emergency contact details, application form, offer letter, subsequent letters written to and from the employee. National Insurance number, payment details and changes in salary. Time off for holidays and sickness.

There are many companies from whom you can buy printed personnel files to hold the employee's details. It is also wise to hold details of payment (tax, SSP, SMP) on separate cards or cards that can be withdrawn from the personnel file. HM Inspectors are not allowed access to the other details and perhaps shouldn't have total access to the personnel file which should be treated as confidential. If requested to show inspectors details of pay, statutory sick pay and maternity pay, these can be withdrawn from the file. This therefore maintains confidentiality of other information held on the employee.

Reference book

We have referred to various papers that should be kept for reference, i.e. policies and procedures. We have outlined in this chapter examples of various reference documents that you could use and adapt for your own reference manual. The firm's reference manual does not have to be a published book, but can be a folder with pages that can be replaced and updated when necessary. This is probably the ideal reference book as policies may change or new policies may need to be added or amended. As a rough outline, we have listed below the papers that should be in the reference folder. This folder should be available to employees on request or should be displayed prominently so that employees can refer to it as and when needed. This is particularly important for grievance and disciplinary procedures.

Reference book contents

- Holiday entitlement/pay
- Holiday entitlement/calculation
- Sickness and injury procedures
- Grievance and appeal procedures
- Disciplinary and dismissal procedures
- Examples of disciplinary regulations and reasons for dismissal
- Periods of notice
- Confidentiality and conflicts of interest (where appropriate)
- General information
- Company cars (where appropriate)
- Maternity leave
- Jury service
- Health and safety policy
- Policy on trade unions (where appropriate)
- Data Protection Act (where appropriate)
- Equal opportunities statement.

9 Guide to employment law

Recruiting staff □ Paying people and hours of work □ Health and Safety at work □ Computerizing information □ Employee relations □ Terminating staff contracts □ Employee rights at a glance □ Why take out insurance?

In this chapter you will find a brief overview of the mass of employment law that surrounds employing people. It is essential that you understand the legal implications of employing people and that you keep up to date with changes in the law.

Many organizations have already developed employers' handbooks on employment law that are continuously updated. A concise and easy-to-understand reference book has been developed by Croner Publications Ltd. It is entitled *Croner's Reference Book for Employers* and you are urged to obtain a copy of this or a similar publication. Copies can be obtained from: Croner Publications Ltd, Croner House, 173 Kingston Road, New Malden, Surrey KT3 3SS.

For ease of reference this chapter has been divided into three main sections: the legal aspects surrounding the recruitment of staff, the legal aspects of employing staff and the legal aspects of the termination of staff contracts. There is obvious overlap between these three areas. The legal implications of employing people have been dealt with throughout the book and you should refer to the appropriate chapter, if you are interested in a particular area of management.

Recruiting staff

Figure 9.1 provides a basic overview of the main legal implications of recruitment.

Who can you recruit?

There are provisions surrounding the employment of young persons which regulate the hours and age of young people in certain employments.

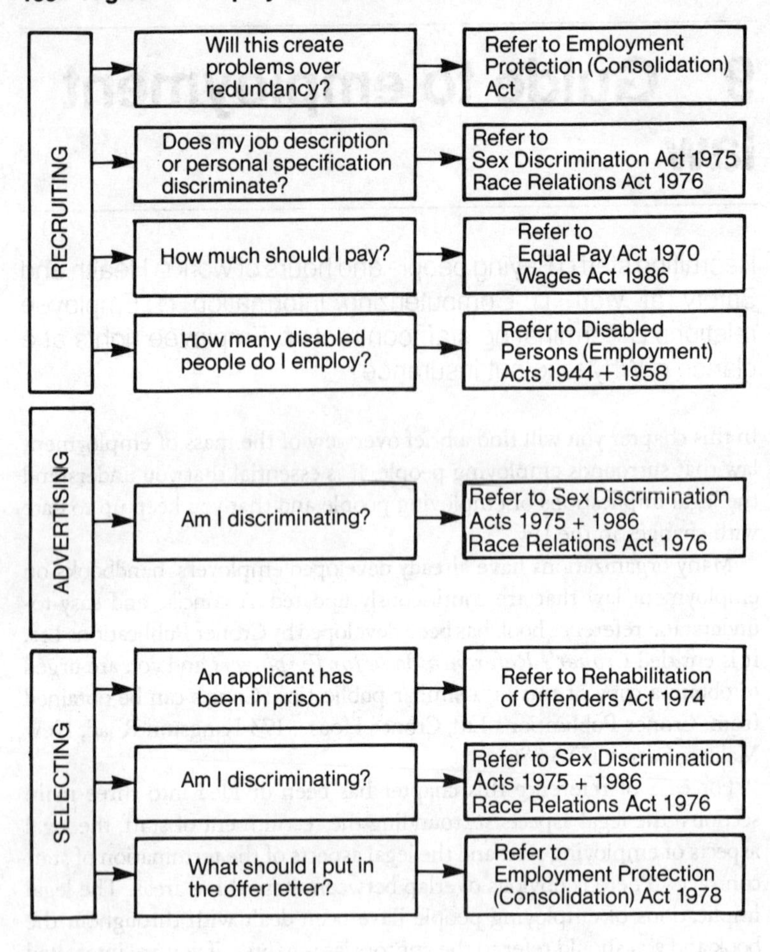

Fig. 9.1 The legal implications of recruitment

Please refer to the Young Persons (Employment) Acts 1938 and 1964 and the Factories Act 1961.

Young people are defined as those of either sex over the compulsory school age who have not reached the age of 18. In England and Wales, pupils who have their sixteenth birthday between 1 September and 31 January can leave at the end of the Spring term. Pupils who have their sixteenth birthday between 1 February and 31 August can leave on or after the Friday preceding the Spring Bank holiday. In Scotland the leaving dates are determined by the Secretary of State.

Individuals of the state retirement age may be employed in certain circumstances. However individuals may lose certain protection rights (refer to Employment Protection (Consolidation) Act 1978) and employers will still be liable for secondary National Insurance contributions.

If you are currently making someone redundant, you should refer to the Employment Protection (Consolidation) Act 1978 regarding how to handle recruitment during this period. You should also refer to the Sex Discrimination Act 1975 and the Race Relations Act 1976.

Are you required to employ disabled people?

If you are currently employing less than three per cent disabled staff in your organization, you should refer to the Disabled Persons (Employment) Acts 1944 and 1958. If you employ less than twenty people, you are not liable under the Act.

What rights do job applicants have?

Job applicants have the right not to be discriminated against on the grounds of sex or race. If you need to go into this in detail, please refer to relevant Acts. If an individual feels that he has been discriminated against during the selection, advertising or interview procedures, he or she has the right to apply to an industrial tribunal for compensation within three months of the incident. Application forms and clear reasons for rejection of a candidate should therefore be kept for a minimum of three months to enable you to refer to these.

Should you recruit ex-criminals?

If an individual has 'spent' his or her conviction, that person does not have to admit to the offence on an application form or in an interview. You cannot technically deny individuals employment on the grounds of spent convictions, although at the end of the day the Courts cannot compel engagement). Any offence leading to imprisonment will take at least seven years to spend, and a period of over two and a half years in prison is never spent. If serious problems arise in this area, you may need to refer to the Rehabilitation of Offenders Act 1974.

Are contracts of employment necessary?

A contract will be seen to exist whether or not it is in writing between yourself and the employee as soon as he or she agrees to start work. The contract becomes effective when terms and conditions have been agreed. Care should be taken therefore during the interview not to 'promise' and 'agree' aspects of the contract that later will not be offered. If this is the case, the contract will be deemed to be broken.

What information has to be provided in writing?

Those working over sixteen hours a week, or who have worked over eight hours a week for five years, must receive the following items within thirteen weeks of entering employment:

- the employer's name
- job title
- date employment began
- amount of pay, sick pay, pensions (if applicable)
- hours of work, holiday entitlement
- length of notice required
- disciplinary rules
- methods of raising problems.

You are obliged to provide an itemised statement of employees' pay showing:

- gross amount
- variable deductions (e.g., income tax)
- fixed deductions (e.g., pensions)
- net pay.

Additional items may be inserted into the contract as the company requires, for example, restrictions on working for competitors.

How can contracts be changed?

If any part of the contract changes, the affected individual(s) must be informed in writing within a month of the change. Normally changes can only be made with the consent of the employee.

How should contractual information be communicated?

- A statement of basic personal details given in writing to each employee
- Appointment letters to new employees
- Reference documents on pay, conditions of work, etc., which should be accessible to all affected employees.

See Chap. 8.

Paying people and hours of work

(See also Chap. 4.)

Are there any legal requirements affecting the amount you pay?

Generally, it is up to you to set the rate of pay, although if you recognize a trade union you will need to take account of local and national agreements.

Wages councils

In wages council industries, you can be fined if you do not pay the established minimum hourly and overtime rates, or provide the minimum holiday entitlement. Individuals under the age of 21 are not covered by wages council provisions.

Equal pay

You should pay equal amounts to men and women engaged on 'like work' (the same employment) or 'work of equal value' (work which, in terms of demands made on the employee, e.g., effort, skill and decision making, is equivalent). A tribunal could require you to put right inequalities should an individual make a complaint.

What deductions should be made?

You should deduct tax from pay at source (PAYE) for all employees. Your local tax office will advise you as to how much to deduct and will provide tax codes.

Class 1 National Insurance contributions for both the employer and for each employee should be made to the Collector of Taxes. The employee's contribution can be deducted from his or her pay. Contact the Inland Revenue or DHSS for further information.

Do you have to pay people when they are sick?

There is a legal requirement for paying staff who are sick who qualify under certain conditions. For further information on statutory sick pay, please refer to Chap. 4.

Should you provide maternity payment?

(See also Chap. 4.)
If a woman has over two years service with you (or has worked between 8 and 16 hours a week for 5 years), she is normally entitled to:

- 90% of normal pay for the first six weeks of her absence, less the flat rate maternity allowance. You can claim this back from the Government's Maternity Fund.
- Return to her former job, or a suitable alternative, provided she gives you notice of her intention before her absence and confirms this 21 days before her return.

The job should be held open for up to 29 weeks following the woman's confinement if she wishes to return.

If you have less than five employees, you can legitimately claim that it is not feasible to take back the employee. Staff should be made fully aware of maternity arrangements through suitable communication methods.

On what grounds can employees take time off work?

Employees can take reasonable time off to:

- attend antenatal clinics (paid)
- look for work if declared redundant with at least two years' service (paid)
- public duties (for employees who hold public positions, such as magistrates; members of local authorities; members of industrial tribunals; and members of certain health, education, water, and river authorities), jury service, etc. (sometimes paid)
- attend training courses for safety representatives (paid)
- carry out trade union duties, where a trade union is recognized (unpaid). (Paid for members of staff who are union officials.)

Health and safety at work

What are your major responsibilities?

- To inform your local authority or the Health and Safety Executive that you are employing people (if they are employed in an office, shop or factory).

- If you employ five or more employees, to draw up a basic policy statement stressing the firm's absolute commitment to ensuring healthy and safe working conditions and specifying how this commitment will be carried out in practice. The content of statements should be effectively communicated to those affected.
- To provide a safe place of work and safe equipment within the constraints of what you can afford and the size of risks involved.
- To inform employees of the arrangements that have been made in connection with the provision of first aid, including the location of equipment, facilities of personnel.
- To maintain the appropriate number of trained First Aiders, if over fifty employees. If under fifty employees to maintain an appointed person for first aid. To keep and update a book reporting on accidents at work.
- To provide employees with information on matters relating to their health and safety and to train them in safe working practices.
- To provide time off for employee safety representatives to devote to safety matters.
- To set up a safety committee for discussion of safety matters and implementing improvements, if this is requested by two or more representatives
- To complete form F2508 (available from Her Majesty's Stationery Office) if an individual is incapacitated for three or more consecutive days due to an accident at work and to send this to the Health and Safety Executive within seven days. The three-day consecutive period does not include the day of the accident but does include days not normally worked, including weekends.
- To immediately inform the Health and Safety Executive of major accidents that occur at work, e.g., death, loss of limb, loss of eye, etc.

Inspectors have wide powers to implement health and safety legislation, and failure to comply can result in fines or imprisonment. Please refer to the Health and Safety at work Act 1974.

Are there any special exemptions for the small firm?

As noted above, if you employ less than five people, you are exempted from the requirement to provide a written policy statement.

Computerizing information

What are the restrictions?

On 12 July 1984 the Data Protection Act received the royal assent and passed on to the statute book. It is the first piece of legislation in the United Kingdom to address the use of computers and its purpose is to protect information about individuals and to enforce a set of standards for the processing of such information. The Act regulates the use of automatically processed information relating to individuals and the provision of services in respect of such information. The Act does *not* therefore cover the processing of personal data by manual methods, nor does it cover information relating to corporate bodies.

Under the Act data users must adhere to certain principles in connection with the personal data they hold.

- The information should be collected and processed fairly and lawfully.
- The information should be held for specified, lawful registered purposes.
- The information should be used for only registered purposes or disclosed to registered recipients.
- The information should be adequate and relevant for the purposes for which it is held.
- The information should be accurate and where appropriate up to date.
- The information should not be held longer than necessary for the stated purpose.
- Individuals have certain rights to access information held on them.
- This information should have appropriate security surrounding it.

Data users must register with the Data Protection Registrar which involves a small subscription. You are a data user if you hold personal information on any storage system of wordprocessing or computerized equipment. Some areas such as payroll information are exempt from the Act. You should contact the Data Protection Register for further information to obtain the relevant registration forms and to ascertain if you are exempt. This is vitally important as failure to comply with the Act can be a criminal offence and involve imprisonment for offenders.

Employee relations

See Chapter 6.

Terminating staff contracts

(See also Chap. 7.)

The employer or the employee can lawfully terminate the contract by giving the required notice period. If the employee fails to work his or her period of notice there is actually little you can do about it. Your redress is via the county courts, which can be in practice an expensive measure.

If you fail to give correct notice to the employee, you will be held to have 'wrongfully' dismissed the employee and the employee has the right to claim compensation via the county courts.

What are the employment rights of part-time and temporary employees?

Temporary employees have the same rights as other employees providing they meet the statutory requirements where necessary and work the minimum number of hours (see relevant chapters).

Exceptions apply to those replacing women on maternity leave, or those replacing individuals who have been suspended on medical grounds.

Part-time workers will be eligible for most statutory protection if:

- they work over 16 hours per week, or
- they have been engaged for five years continuously and have worked at least eight hours per week.

What are my major responsibilities regarding redundancy?

(See also Chap. 7.)

- To inform the Redundancy Notification Office of the Department of Employment at least 30 days in advance if you intend to make ten or more staff redundant. If the figure of staff to be made redundant exceeds 100, then notice to the Secretary of State should be given 90 days' prior to the first dismissal.
- To provide employees who have at least two years' service with a redundancy payment according to their age and length of service.
- To provide at least two days' paid leave of absence to redundant employees to search for another job (provided they have at least two years' service).
- If possible, to provide suitable alternative employment and to avoid compulsory redundancy.
- To provide redundant employees with as much notice as possible.

- If you recognize a trade union, to discuss redundancy proposals with a union representative. If ten or more staff are to be made redundant, at least thirty days' notice must be given to the union. It must also be provided with information on reasons for redundancy, numbers and descriptions of those to be made redundant, proposed method of selection, method and timing of dismissals.

Are there any special exceptions regarding redundancies for the small firm?

Where less than ten people are to be made redundant at one place of work there is no requirement to give advance notice to the Department of Employment.

Firms employing less than ten people are eligible to claim a rebate from the Department of Employment.

What are the rights of staff when the business is transferred or merged?

Staff have the right to be transferred automatically on the same terms without loss of service or related rights.

What is dismissal?

(See also Chap. 7.)
Dismissal occurs either when you terminate the individual's contract, when a fixed term contract expires or when you act in such a way that you effectively break a major contractual term, and the individual has no option but to resign.

A person who feels he or she is dismissed unfairly may qualify to take the case to an industrial tribunal which can order you to pay damages or to take the individual back, although in the last resort reinstatement cannot be compelled.

When is a dismissal fair?

This depends a great deal on the circumstances, but it is essential to follow a disciplinary procedure. Dismissal should take place as the last resort.

Dismissal must be for one of the specified fair reasons:

- redundancy – when the firm no longer requires work of the type done by the employee, i.e. it is the worker's job that becomes redundant, not the worker.

- lack of capability, lack of relevant qualifications, ill health – this would usually arise at the beginning of employment when it becomes clear that the employee cannot do the job because of lack of skill or mental or physical ill-health.
- misconduct – this will very much depend on the circumstances of each case, but the following are usually relevant: imcompetence; neglect; disobedience (e.g. assault on other employees); morality; drunkenness.
- where the employee could not continue to work in the position without breaking the law, for example when a driver is banned from driving for a drink-driving offence.
- some other substantial reason which satisfies an industrial tribunal.

If you dismiss someone for being a member of a trade union, and for taking part in trade union activities, the dismissal will automatically be unfair.

Are there any special exceptions regarding dismissal for the small firm?

Tribunals will take into account the size and administrative resources of the firm when deciding whether or not a dismissal is unfair.

If it is not feasible, you will not be obliged to provide written warnings, a right of appeal, or to conduct full scale investigations.

Additionally:

- you are not required to have formal procedures when dismissing for ill health
- tribunals are likely to hold that small firms are entitled to expect the highest standards of conduct, and that they should be allowed considerable flexibility to vary contracts of employment.

Who qualifies to take a case to an industrial tribunal?

- Individuals who have been discriminated against on the grounds of sex and/or race. There is no qualifying service requirement if discrimination occurs on these grounds. Individuals who are not yet employed may also qualify.
- A woman dismissed solely on the grounds of pregnancy. Again there is no service qualification.
- Full-time staff employed for two years or more or part-time staff working sixteen hours or more a week for five or more years.

9

Employee rights at a glance

	Employees working 8 hrs or less per week	Employees working 8-15 hrs per week	Employees working over 16 hrs per week
Not to be discriminated against on the grounds of sex or marital status	✓	✓	✓
Not to be discriminated against on the grounds of race	✓	✓	✓
Not to be victimized against for taking part in Union activities	✓	✓	✓
Statement of terms of employment (within 13 weeks service)	—	—	✓
Time off for public duties	—	—	✓
Itemized pay statement	—	—	✓
Time off as official of recognised independent trade union	—	—	✓
Time off to take part in activities of independent trade union	—	—	✓
Time off to perform function as safety representative	—	—	✓
Minimum period of notice	—	5 years	1 month
Guarantee payment	—	5 years	1 month
Pay during suspension on medical grounds	—	5 years	1 month
Not to be unfairly dismissed	—	5 years	2 years
Not to be dismissed because of pregnancy	—	5 years	2 years
Written statement for reasons for dismissal	6 months	6 months	6 months
Maternity pay Lower Rate	—	5 years	26 weeks
Maternity pay Higher Rate	—	5 years	2 years
Maternity leave and right to return	—	5 years	2 years
Redundancy payment	2 years	2 years	2 years

* Could be construed as sex discrimination.

One month = one calendar month one year = twelve calendar months

Fig. 9.2 Employee rights at a glance

If your firm employs under twenty people and has done so during the two- (or five-) year period, then individuals will not have the right to apply to an industrial tribunal.

Employee rights at a glance

Figure 9.2 gives you an easy reference guide to employee rights.

Why take out insurance?

There are two main reasons why you should take out insurance cover. The first is a *legal* requirement. The second reason is best described as *peace of mind.* If you are not insured and a catastrophe strikes it could mean the loss of your business, no matter how well you are doing, and, in some cases, the loss of your home, to help pay for damages. You should pay particular attention to your house and contents insurance if you run your business from home, as the insurance cover you are likely to have is a householder's policy and does not apply to the running of your own business. You should make sure therefore, in this situation, that you take out a commercial policy.

What do I have to insure legally?

Employers' liability

Under the Employers' Liability (Compulsory Insurance) Act 1969 all employers must insure against personal injury and disease sustained by their employees and arising out of, or in the course of, their employment. The insurance must be made under an approved policy with an authorised insurer. A certificate of insurance will be issued and a copy of this must be displayed for the benefit of all employees at each place of work (see Fig. 9.3). The amount of insurance that must be taken out should be at least two million pounds in respect of any claim that may arise. In many cases these policies give unlimited cover.

Any employee, i.e., 'an individual who has entered into or works under a contract of service (employment) or apprenticeship with an employer whether by way of manual labour, clerical or otherwise, whether such contract is express or implied, oral or in writing', is covered by this legal requirement. The following persons do not have to be insured:

- an employee who is related to you (the employer) as a husband, wife,

Certificate of Employers' Liability Insurance

(A copy or copies of this certificate must be displayed at each place of business at which the policyholder employs persons covered by the policy.)

Policy No.__________

1. NAME OF POLICYHOLDER
2. DATE OF COMMENCEMENT OF INSURANCE
3. DATE OF EXPIRY OF INSURANCE

We hereby certify that the policy to which this certificate relates satisfies the requirements of relevant law applicable in Great Britain, Northern Ireland, the Isle of Man, the Island of Jersey, the Island of Guernsey and the Island of Alderney or to offshore installations in territorial waters around Great Britain and its Continental Shelf.

(Authorised Insurers)

On behalf of the Board

Fig. 9.3 A certificate of employers' liability insurance showing the information that has to be displayed.

father, mother, grandfather, grandmother, stepfather, stepmother, son, daughter, grandson, granddaughter, stepson, stepdaughter, brother, sister, half-brother or half-sister

- an individual who is employed in a private household, e.g., nanny, gardener, etc.
- an employee who does not usually live in the UK and is working for you for less than 14 days.

You will only be exempt from the requirements to insure under the Act if you fall into one of the following categories:

1. Local authorities (other than parish council).
2. Boards or committees whose members include a local authority representative.
3. Police authorities.
4. Nationalised industries.
5. Crews of ships & hovercrafts if insured with a mutual insurance association of ship owners.
6. Certain bodies financed out of public funds.

There are *no* other exceptions. The fine for failure to comply with this Act can be up to £1,000, and up to £400 if the certificate is not displayed or not available on the request of the Health and Safety Executive.

It is important to note that care should be taken if individuals who are not defined as 'employees' work on the premises. These include contractors and, in some cases, work experience trainees. In the case of the latter, you should ensure that the party responsible for their safety has taken out insurance on their behalf. Whenever possible request this in writing to reduce your liability for these individuals.

Motor insurance

If your business has any company vehicles you should make sure that the insurance covers them for business use. You are required under the Road Traffic Act to have insurance in order to pay out, if you are liable, for any injury caused by one of your vehicles to other people, including passengers. As a minimum you should have third party cover. Failure to tell the insurance company that vehicles are used for business purposes may mean it will not pay out if you have an accident. You should ensure that all employees who use the vehicles are covered by the insurance policy.

Equipment

By law, certain equipment (e.g., pressure vessels, lifting tackle and lifts) has to be inspected at regular intervals to ensure that it is safe for your employees to use. You can combine the maintenance contract with an insurance policy to cover you against the risk of explosion, accidental damage, and breakdown. This is not a legal requirement, however, it would be seen by employees as you taking a 'caring approach' towards their welfare by ensuring that in the event of an accident they will receive more compensation than the basic minimum.

What other types of insurance are advisable?

Public liability

Although not a legal requirement, public liability insurance is strongly recommended. This applies no matter how small your business. For instance, what happens if you employ an electrician who repairs a client's kettle and the client later receives a bad shock, or worse, is killed, because of the incorrect wiring of that kettle? The main point about public liability insurance is that it provides cover for your legal liability to anyone should you or your staff inflict accidental damage or injury.

Professional indemnity

If you are providing a service you should consider taking out professional indemnity insurance for yourself and your employees. Doctors, solicitors, accountants and chartered surveyors automatically take out professional indemnity insurance to ensure that in the event of their advice being inaccurate, or harmful to their client, they will be protected against any claims. Such insurance usually saves the cost of solicitors' fees, and any award made against you or your employees. Professional indemnity insurance is very expensive as claims are increasing every year; you should, however, examine this option closely if you are in a service business.

'Key man' insurance

This can be taken out in respect of one individual, for instance, yourself as the owner, or other key members of your team. This policy provides a lump sum that is paid to the company in the event of the vital manager/ executive dying.

As a small business owner it is very tempting to assume immediately that you need a 'key man' policy. However, you should consider the following before opting for one, weighing up the cost of premiums against the eventual gain for the business itself. Ask yourself whether a lump sum introduced into the business in the event of the death of the key person will actually help to continue to operate the business? Is it possible, for example, to stay in business as a fashion house without a chief designer? If the business will not benefit by such a policy in the long-term, it may not be worth having this type of insurance.

Permanent health insurance

Permanent health insurance can be taken out for all employees to insure them against sickness and accidents, and to protect their salary during such times. This scheme is of particular advantage to the small business, as the loss of a member of staff for long periods may mean having to pay salary twice for temporary cover, which can cause financial problems for the firm.

In many small businesses where there are close working relationships with staff you may feel that you are morally bound to continue payment. Taking out permanent health insurance can ensure that employees continue to be paid for long periods of absence (besides statutory sickness payments) without financial repercussion for the small business. This can also be seen as an additional benefit by employees and gives greater security to individuals.

Private health insurance

Many companies now offer their executives and staff a private health plan for themselves and sometimes their families as well – with BUPA or PPP, or a similar organization. This benefit is taxable and provides comfort for your staff and their families.

The advantage to the company can be seen in the fact that health care is available in emergencies and can also be at the company's convenience for routine sickness. It ensures that employees receive prompt treatment – they can be treated quickly and efficiently and put back to work in the shortest possible time.

The cost of private health insurance can often be high. Again, employees view company schemes as an additional benefit. Discount is often available for group membership schemes.

Theft by employees/fidelity guarantee

In addition to your general insurance policies against theft you can also, for a small extra premium, be covered against theft by your employees. You will need to be able to demonstrate that you have very tight security systems in order to get this insurance. Although you may know your team well this type of insurance is worth considering.

Where do I buy insurance?

You will probably need the services of an insurance broker. You should ensure that they are registered with the Insurance Brokers Registration Council, as the council requires brokers to behave in accordance with a code of conduct. Brokers can in theory deal with a wide variety of insurance, however, in practice many tend to deal with only a few key sources. It is worthwhile, therefore, obtaining quotes from three brokers and examining the proposals before taking out an insurance policy. Insurance brokers are paid on commission for the insurance cover and should not, therefore, charge you an arrangement fee. Check carefully beforehand that no fee is required.

Index